# Challenging Standards

# Challenging Standards

## Navigating Conflict
## and Building Capacity
## in the Era of the Common Core

Jonathan A. Supovitz and James P. Spillane

ROWMAN & LITTLEFIELD
Lanham • Boulder • New York • London

Published by Rowman & Littlefield
A wholly owned subsidiary of The Rowman & Littlefield Publishing Group, Inc.
4501 Forbes Boulevard, Suite 200, Lanham, Maryland 20706
www.rowman.com

Unit A, Whitacre Mews, 26-34 Stannary Street, London SE11 4AB

British Library Cataloguing in Publication Information Available

**Library of Congress Cataloging-in-Publication Data**

Challenging standards : navigating conflict and building capacity in the era of the common core / edited by Jonathan A. Supovitz and James Spillane.
pages cm.
Includes bibliographical references.
ISBN 978-1-4758-1584-9 (cloth : alk. paper) — ISBN 978-1-4758-1585-6 (pbk. : alk. paper) — ISBN 978-1-4758-1586-3 (electronic) 1. Common Core State Standards (Education) 2. Education—Standards—United States—States. I. Supovitz, Jonathan A., editor of compilation. II. Spillane, James P., editor of compilation.
LB3060.83.C435 2015
379.1'580973—dc23

2015013054

♾ ™ The paper used in this publication meets the minimum requirements of American National Standard for Information Sciences Permanence of Paper for Printed Library Materials, ANSI/NISO Z39.48-1992.

Printed in the United States of America

# Contents

# About the Consortium for Policy Research in Education (CPRE)

The Consortium for Policy Research in Education (CPRE) brings together education experts from renowned research institutions to contribute new knowledge that informs PK–20 education policy and practice. Our work is peer-reviewed and open-access.

CPRE **conducts** program evaluation, applied research, qualitative and quantitative methods, advance survey techniques, and data analysis for federal, state, and foundational grants; **connects** policymakers and practitioners to evidence-based knowledge and research findings from CPRE researchers and others in the field; and, **collaborates** with policymakers, practitioners, and researchers to improve PK–20 educational policy through partnering and serving as thought-partners to inform their decision-making.

CPRE's member institutions include: University of Pennsylvania, Graduate School of Education; Teachers College, Columbia University; Harvard University, Graduate School of Education; Stanford University, Graduate School of Education; University of Michigan, School of Education; University of Wisconsin–Madison, School of Education; and, Northwestern University, School of Education and Social Policy.

# Preface

The idea for this book grew out of a February 2014 meeting of educational researchers in Philadelphia, Pennsylvania, that was sponsored by the American Educational Research Association. The meeting was organized to discuss the educational policies and political environment surrounding the introduction of the Common Core State Standards. The attendees were chosen to participate because they had investigated different aspects of past education reform initiatives over their careers. As the meeting grew more animated it became clear that we had so much to share with practitioners about our experiences studying the implementation of major reforms in American education.

Our goal in this book is to invert the typical way that researchers report what they have learned. Researchers are often more comfortable writing from the data of very specific research studies and tend to become more tentative as we generalize beyond our specific findings. But for this book we charged the authors to flip the traditional script. We asked each author to speak from their accumulated wisdom to the challenge of standards implementation. We guided the authors with the following charge:

> You have been studying education reform and implementation for a long time and this is a rare opportunity for you to share your accumulated knowledge with educational leaders. Start with a big challenge or big idea in your area of expertise and imagine you are sitting at a table with a group of influential school/district/state leaders and you have this opportunity to make two to three key points from your accumulated experience to help them with the big challenge of standards implementation. What are the key messages that you want to share? What wisdom will benefit educational leaders the most?

As you can tell from the directive above, the primary audience for this book is school, district, and state education leaders. This includes district administrators, coordinators, and coaches, as well as school principals and teacher leaders—basically anyone who is interested in implementation *beyond* the individual classroom. Our ambition is to take you out of your immediate context for a few brief moments and share with you some of our accrued understanding of meeting the challenge posed by ambitious standards in an era of high accountability and partisan politics.

Finally, the chapters in this book are designed to be read and discussed by groups of educational leaders, leadership teams, or within professional learning communities. For this reason, each section introduction poses a series of questions and discussion points for connecting the chapters back to your local situations and contexts.

The authors would like to thank the American Educational Research Association (AERA) for sponsoring a conference on the Policy and Politics of the Common Core. It was during that conference that the idea for this book was germinated. The authors would also like to thank Jackie Kerstetter, the Communications Director of the Consortium for Policy Research in Education, for expertly facilitating communication amongst the authors and developing promotional plans for this book. Additionally, the authors are indebted to education leaders William Gretzula, Linda Grobman, and Dennis Perry for providing sage feedback from the practitioner perspective during draft presentations of many of these chapters. Finally, we would like to thank Tom Koerner and Carlie Wall of Rowman & Littlefield for championing this book.

Jonathan A. Supovitz and James P. Spillane
March 2015

# Introduction

## Jonathan A. Supovitz and James P. Spillane

Educators can become so engrossed in the challenges of their daily work that there is little time to step back and consider some fundamental questions about how their work fits into the larger picture of educational improvement and how it has come to be organized as it is. This book invites you to do so by providing you with a variety of perspectives to help you navigate conflict and build capacity for school improvement in the era of the Common Core State Standards.

It's easy to see why standards are considered as a major organizing scheme for education: Standards define expectations for teachers and students; they help to guide what content teachers are expected to focus on at each grade level; they influence textbook content, curricular choices, and pacing decisions; and they are a major influence on what is tested. Standards are also intended to catalyze greater coherence among all these elements in the highly decentralized American education system through the signals they send to both educators and the wider market of education support resources. Even so, there is a long distance between the intentions of standards and the practices in schools and classrooms.

This introductory chapter frames the essays to come by laying out the contemporary arguments for standards, the evolution of standards-based policies in American education, and the contested educational priorities and issues they raise. Ultimately, as all the authors in this book attest, standards-based reform will only be as effective as educators are able to organize the systems within their purview to use it to foster productive educational experiences for students.

This is America's second major go-around with standards-based reform in the past twenty-five years. Why have policymakers returned to standards as the key lever for change? There are certainly other approaches that policy setters could use to reform the American education system. In fact, we are just coming out of an experience with test-based accountability as a fulcrum for change. If we are going to engage again with standards-based reform, what makes the current movement any more promising than the last?

Policymaking is the craft of building systems that direct peoples' attention and behavior in certain (ideally) predictable and productive ways. This is your bailiwick. Regardless of the level of the education system at which you operate, you are a policymaker because the decisions you make influence the activities of those around you. But, out of all the possible ways that leaders of governing bodies (at the federal, state, or local levels) could exercise their limited, but powerful influence through directives, signals, and incentives (both positive and negative), why have we returned to standards as the organizing principle for reform? We see at least seven reasons for a focus on standards as a catalyst for change in American education.

First, standards represent the effort of policymakers to *define academic expectations* for educators all up and down the education system. While there is much contestation about the purposes of schooling, literacy and numeracy and a basic knowledge of how contemporary government and society operate is a largely agreed-upon mission of schools. Having a clear and generally accepted set of outcomes seems essential for any improvement effort, even as this goal has been difficult to achieve due to the fact that educational expectations are so intertwined with contested fundamental values.

Second, standards are an attempt to *influence the core classroom interactions between teachers and students*. There is a long tradition of structural reforms in education that have changed the organizations surrounding classrooms but have failed to influence the central dynamics of classroom teaching and learning. The instructional core has long been viewed as resilient to change, despite repeated efforts to introduce instructional reforms. Exactly because standards focus teachers and schools on specific student outcomes, they are viewed as a catalyst to change students' learning opportunities and experiences.

Third, standards reform represents *a response to the prevailing perception of America's mediocre educational performance*. This view of undistinguished performance has been an overriding perception about American education since at least the Nation at Risk report of 1983 which famously began, "The educational foundations of our society are presently being eroded by a rising tide of mediocrity that threatens our very future as a Nation and a people" (Gardner et al., 1983).

Flat longitudinal performance on the National Assessment of Educational Progress (NAEP) and middling performance on international comparative assessments such as Trends in International Mathematics and Science Study (TIMSS) and the Programme for International Student Assessment (PISA) have perpetuated this belief and spurred efforts to improve education.

Fourth, standards are seen as *a statement of commitment to equity* in education and society. By holding common expectations for all students, standards signal that opportunities are equal for all students, teachers, and schools, regardless of economic circumstance, ethnic affiliation, or racial heritage. Relatedly, common standards potentially make it easier for high-mobility students (usually students living in poverty) to keep up with school, because the curriculum should be relatively similar across contexts organized under common standards. Fifth, by developing a common set of expectations, *standards help to build a common knowledge base for teachers* around a particular set of academic skills. A common knowledge base, the theory goes, should help teacher training programs, curriculum providers, and assessment developers to build high-quality support materials, and can facilitate on-the-job professional learning.

Sixth, and related, standards might *focus the professional conversation among educators*, thereby potentially enabling greater teacher professional learning about instruction. Standards might do so by providing a common focus and a familiar language for discussing instructional practice and devising ways of improving it.

Finally, standards might help to lay the groundwork for markets to work more effectively in the education sector. By specifying what students should know and be able to do in core school subjects across the nation and using commonly accepted assessments, the new standards system has the potential to create "common" performance metrics that can be used by clients (e.g., parents and students) to compare schools and make decisions about good schools for their children.

Thus, there are a whole host of rationales for using standards as an organizing principle to catalyze productive educational change. Many of these arguments motivated the standards-based reform efforts of the 1990s. This effort was built around three general principles. First, standards developed by each state would provide a set of targets of what kids ought to know and be able to do at each grade from kindergarten through twelfth grade. Second, states would measure progress toward standards by developing aligned assessments that incorporated rewards and sanctions for holding educators accountable for meeting the standards. And third, states would provide districts and schools local flexibility to build and organize their capacity as they saw fit to meet the academic expectations (Smith & O'Day, 1991). This structure of clear goals (i.e., standards), measures (assessments), and incentives (accountability) at the state level, combined with decentralized implementation latitude, fit well with our historical tradition of local education control.

But theory often plays out differently in practice, and this rendition of standards-based reform was generally seen as disappointing. It led each state to develop its own standards and assessment systems, which were of uneven quality and rigor. The associated state tests were also of uneven caliber and difficulty. Further still, political pressure often pushed states to adjust the passing rates of their test scores to avoid the public backlash that comes with drops in performance. Further, policymakers learned that standards and assessments by themselves did not catalyze the capacity necessary to develop the strong educational infrastructure necessary to meet the standards.

The 2000s gave rise to the era of test-based accountability in education. The 2001 passage of the No Child Left Behind (NCLB) Act inaugurated an expansion of testing by requiring states that received federal Title I funds to assess students in all grades between third and eighth, and one year in high school. NCLB pressed states to develop plans to have all schools make adequate yearly progress with a target of 100 percent proficiency by 2014—an endeavor that proved to be impossible. The NCLB legislation also required states to disaggregate their results by subgroups in an effort to prevent districts and schools from hiding disparities in performance within overall averages. This movement can be seen as an attempt to tighten the linkages in the theory of standards-based reform by increasing student performance expectations via high-stakes testing to hold schools accountable for meeting standards.

Research on schools pressed by test-based accountability showed both productive and unproductive responses. There was an increase in attention to tested subjects, a rise in test preparation behavior, more attention to students just at the cusp of passing the test, and greater attention to heretofore marginalized students (Hamilton, 2003). But some states also gamed the system by creating tests that most students could easily pass. There were also several cases of systematic cheating by educators in school districts and schools that made national headlines. The accountability emphasis of No Child Left Behind left many policymakers convinced that although pressure was important, we couldn't just squeeze higher performance out of the system—we had to build a structure to support it.

This brings us to the current major reform initiative in the United States: the Common Core State Standards (CCSS), or as they are sometimes rebranded, the College- and Career-Ready Standards. The CCSS set forth what student should know and be able to do in mathematics and English language arts (ELA) at each grade level. In a remarkable moment of bipartisanship, the CCSS were adopted in 2010 by the legislatures in forty-six states and the District of Columbia. Alaska, Texas, Virginia, and Nebraska did not adopt the Common Core, preferring their own state standards. Minnesota adopted the Common Core ELA standards, but not those in mathematics. Since then, the CCSS have become remarkably politicized and several states have either backed away from the CCSS and/or the associated tests or are in the midst of heated discussions about their involvement with the CCSS.

The standards contain a distinctive set of features. They seek to bring about instructional change by asking educators to focus instruction on fewer topics attended to more deeply in mathematics; and on more complex, content-rich nonfiction, as well as fiction, in ELA. Second, in both subjects, the standards encourage teachers to engage students at higher levels of cognitive demand—asking not just for procedural competency but also for conceptual understanding in mathematics and evidence-grounded argumentation in ELA. These design elements were an attempt to address both the spiraling nature of American curriculum, which results in students encountering the same topics repeatedly and never achieving mastery, and the incessant battles over the relative emphasis on procedural learning and higher-order thinking.

The CCSS also incorporate a number of lessons learned from the earlier standards-based reform movement. The Common Core State Standards had "common" in their title because they were designed as a single set of expectations to eliminate the variation in the quality of state standards experienced in the past. Similarly, the Obama administration provided start-up funding for two test consortia—the Smarter Balanced Assessment Consortium and the Partnership for Assessment of Readiness for College and Careers (PARCC)—to create assessments aligned with the CCSS. The experience of the 1990s version of standards taught us that all standards and assessment systems are not equal.

The standards had "state" in their title because they were purposefully developed at the behest of the state governors and chief state school officers to explicitly avoid the fallout of charges of federal intrusion in local education policy (an allegation that came nevertheless after the Obama administration advocated for the CCSS in the Race to the Top funding competition for states to implement education reform).

The context around which the standards are being introduced has also changed. The Internet has dramatically enhanced teachers' and other stakeholders' access to knowledge. In prior eras, instructional materials and professional knowledge were largely filtered through, and controlled by, school districts, who chose the curricular materials and professional development experiences for their teachers. However, the Internet has created a host of opportunities for teachers to identify classroom materials, gain learning opportunities, interact with peers in wider communities, and post and share assessments. One can see this phenomenon playing out with the Common Core, with a host of websites posting CCSS materials and providing teachers with opportunities to share lesson plans and experiences. At the same time, the Internet has made this information available to all, not just professional educators, and provides a forum to help people organize and mobilize around common concerns. In addition to changes in the digital context, the marketplace of support providers and materials is both richer and more dense, which requires a new set of skills for education consumers. Both of these topics are addressed in subsequent chapters in this book.

Last, but not least, the political landscape is also considerably different. We are living in an increasingly polarized political environment in which social media is expanding public voice in political debates. At least partly for this reason, the CCSS has become progressively more controversial, despite its initial bipartisan support. The challenges of implementing standards within such a political atmosphere is a topic that several authors take up in this volume.

New standards. New context. New policy environment. Old challenge. In order for standards-based reform to change instruction inside of classrooms, leaders at all levels of the system will have to take on the perennial challenge of providing meaningful learning opportunities, enabling relationships, and building support structures to deepen understanding of the implications of the standards for instructional practice. It is the central theme of this book that the ultimate judgment of the influence of the CCSS movement will be seen in the ways in which local actors build upon the scaffolding that standards provide. For, despite the theoretical rationale for standards as an organizing system for education reform, standards are far removed from the daily interactions between teachers and students around academic material that constitutes teaching and enables learning. The road from standards to improved student learning is a long and winding one.

Though the adoption of the standards in a bevy of states represents a major policy accomplishment in U.S. education policymaking, the CCSS must still traverse the long and uneven implementation highway that makes up the U.S. school system. The standards still have to navigate the horizontally and vertically segmented education system through both state and local governmental arrangements that by design and default frustrate rather than foster change. There are a host of additional things that need to occur for the introduction of standards to reach down into schools and influence teaching and improve student outcomes. It is the local educators, who are the key architects of the educational infrastructures that will determine whether or not the new standards will have a constructive influence on teaching and learning, for whom this book is written.

This book is organized into four sectional themes. In the first section, the authors take up different aspects of the leadership challenge of organizing systems and schools for standards implementation. Their accounts not only underscore the critical roles of local educators in determining the fate of government educational policy, but also offer some new ways of thinking about implementation. Challenging more conventional notions about implementation as being about following policy prescriptions, these chapters reconceptualize implementation as a learning and sense-making process in which the ideas advanced by standards and their entailments for classroom instruction are constructed by local educators.

The authors of the second section of the book dig deeper into how leaders at different levels of the education system can support teacher enactment of the standards in classrooms—the real epicenters for change. The authors in this section examine critical issues of curriculum selection and implementation, the crafting of professional development experiences for teachers, and the implication of implementing the standards in different contexts. The authors also raise the important questions around the underlying expectations of the standards for instruction for students from different backgrounds and with different cultural experiences.

Schools and school systems will not engage with standards in a vacuum. The multilayered system of education in America necessitates that leaders must both depend on and contend with a host of system and non-system agencies and actors as they implement reform. The authors of the third section of the book examine the connections both within the education system and links to non-system actors like external support providers and digital resources. In particular, the authors explore the opportunities and pitfalls for leaders navigating in the vast, largely unregulated, and uneven environment where there is no shortage of offerings for CCSS-aligned services and materials, most with little evidence to back up their promises. The authors address ways in which schools and school districts can navigate this terrain by engaging with their environment through selective relationships and smart partnering.

Districts and schools are also not insulated from the political environments that envelop them. In section four of the book, the authors describe the landscape of education reform today and sketch the interest groups and positions that dot this landscape. They point out some of the key political issues and sometimes divisive contexts that implementers should understand. The authors assert that political issues that bloom on the surface often have deeper roots, and this section pulls at some of these tendrils to expose the underlying issues and historical causes that help us to better understand how they are manifested today.

Collectively, the essays in this book give you at least three perspectives for *challenging standards*. First, the Common Core standards themselves embody a distinctively high set of expectations for student performance that ratchet up the criteria for both the depth of student knowledge and the facility of understanding. This has a rippling effect across the system, which raises the second challenge of standards—they are a clarion call for professional educators to rethink the surrounding organizations, structures, and relationships that produce the experiences that students receive. This has far-reaching implications for the entire industry: whole school faculties; district central offices; state education departments; higher education institutions who are both the predominant preparers of teachers and leaders as well as the recipients of high school graduates; and the diverse array of material developers and external support providers that contribute capacity to the educational system. The third challenge of standards is the counterforce that remonstrates the existence of the standards themselves. Exactly because education priorities convey societal values, a common set of expectations is bound to raise challenges from those whose preferences are underprioritized. In this triple vortex era of challenging standards educators are tasked with navigating conflict and building capacity for the betterment of the life opportunities of American youth.

## REFERENCES

Gardner, D. P., Larsen, Y. W., Baker, W., & Campbell, A. (1983). *A nation at risk: The imperative for educational reform.* Washington, DC: US Government Printing Office.

Hamilton, L. (2003). Assessment as a policy tool. In Robert Floden (ed.), *Review of Research in Education, 27* 25–68.

Smith, M. S., & O'Day, J. A. (1991). Systemic school reform. In S. H. Fuhrman & B. Malen (eds.), *The politics of curriculum and testing: The 1990 yearbook of the Politics of Education Association* (pp. 233–267). New York: Falmer Press.

*Part 1 Introduction*

# Leading Standards Implementation in Schools and Systems

## James P. Spillane

Despite the ever-increasing presence of state and federal agencies in making policy intended to improve instruction, local conditions remain critical to policy implementation in classrooms and schools (Cohen, 1990; Fullan, 1991). A quarter century of scholarship on the implementation of national and state standards suggests that local educational leaders and teachers are still likely to be the final brokers for CCSS (Firestone, Fitz & Broadfoot, 1999; Spillane, 2004).

Implementation scholarship has increasingly challenged traditional portrayals of instructional policy implementation as a linear process of putting policymakers' ideas into practice. Specifically, researchers have shown how policy implementation involves learning and sense-making about both standards and instruction by both local education leaders and teachers. Putting standards into practice is not just a matter of deciding whether or not to do what standards ask because standards and their accompanying assessments do not offer well-specified scripts or recipes for instruction. Even if they did, local decision makers would still have to make sense of the instructional ideas they are designed to advance. Rather, local implementers engage in a host of sense-making and sense-giving adjustments vis-à-vis standards, as well as with a host of other environmental cues about instruction, that involve figuring out what the instructional ideas entail for them and negotiating how this fits into current instructional practice. Viewed this way, local educational leaders and teachers *construct* ideas about instruction and improving instruction, and negotiate among themselves about these meanings and their validity for their schools and classrooms. The chapters in this section capture some key lessons gleaned from this implementation research on the standards movement.

In chapter 1, Jonathan Supovitz of the University of Pennsylvania argues that leading the challenging work of standards implementation means understanding both its prescriptive and constructive aspects, whose application depends on the tasks involved and the capacities of those who will engage in the work. He raises four questions that leaders should consider in deciding how to engage others in implementation and makes the important connection between standards as a learning challenge for adults as well as students.

In chapter 2, Carol Lee of Northwestern University examines the ways in which the English language arts CCSS both reflect current knowledge in the field about learning processes and miss opportunities to embody recent lessons from research. Taking us inside the standards development process, Lee identifies some of the tensions that the developers faced and how they addressed them. Drawing on experience from the Reading First initiative she identifies several infrastructural components that school systems will need to develop to support standards implementation.

In the third chapter, John Diamond of the University of Wisconsin–Madison identifies three key lessons from implementation research that are especially pertinent when it comes to understanding how the standards are likely to get played out in local school districts and schools. Diamond argues that how the standards influence practice will ultimately depend on how local actors make sense of the instructional ideas advanced through standards, a process that in turn is shaped by a school's organizational resources and capacity as well as the school subject. Diamond lays out five different possible results of local efforts to make sense of standards and their meanings for instruction, and details how organizational resources and circumstances impinge on this process. He also argues for consideration of the multifaceted and subject-specific nature of instruction in any consideration of the implementation challenges facing the CCSS.

In chapter 4, James Spillane of Northwestern University and Megan Hopkins argue for attention to the educational infrastructure with which district policymakers, school leaders, and teachers engage as they make sense of standards and their entailment for instructional practice. They identify several key components of educational infrastructure that guide classroom instruction and structure local efforts to maintain instructional quality and lead instructional improvement. While acknowledging that the educational infrastructure varies from one site to the next, Spillane and Hopkins focus their chapter on how the educational infrastructure varies by school subject even within the same school or school district. Specifically, they argue that some school subjects have more elaborate and well-developed educational infrastructures for supporting instruction, maintaining instructional quality, and leading instructional improvement than other subjects. They argue that these differences are especially consequential when it comes to whether and how schools are likely to engage with making sense of standards and their implications for local practice.

Here are several questions and points for you and your colleagues to discuss to better lead standards implementation in schools and systems:

1. How would you characterize the theory of action for implementation that implicitly or explicitly informs your school and/or district's approach to implementing the CCSS? What aspects are better developed and less developed? What assumptions underlie elements of the logic chain of this theory of action and what will it require to buttress the weakest assumptions?

2. To what extent do the approaches to implementation of the CCSS in your school and/or district actively encourage engagement or sense-making? Based upon your experiences, what do you see as the advantages and constraints of these approaches and how might you capitalize on the former and mitigate the latter?

3. Compare and contrast the educational infrastructure for supporting instruction and instructional improvement in any two core subjects (e.g., English language arts, mathematics, science) in your school and/or district. Identify three key subject-matter differences in the educational infrastructure that are likely to be especially consequential for the implementation of the CCSS and how you might address them.

## Chapter One

# Engaging with Standards

## Jonathan A. Supovitz

One of the most vexing patterns of America's past experiences with ambitious education reform is that initially powerful ideas for change tend to become diluted the more widely they are spread, until what actually gets implemented is a watered-down version of the originally potent idea (Elmore, 1996). This problem is particularly notable for instructional reforms that seek to change the ways that teachers interact with students around particular subject-matter content. The instructional core is a tough nut to crack.

However, this resistance has generally little to do with actual defiance—as the old saying goes, in education, change is the only constant—as much as it has to do with the mindset with which educators encounter reform which, in turn, shapes their response. This chapter examines different ways that educators can approach introducing the Common Core State Standards and argues that how they engage with this learning challenge will have a major impact on their likelihood of making an indelible mark on the future of America's youth.

The underlying logic of the Standards is bold: If we want to achieve dramatically different outcomes, then we need to provide students with fundamentally different learning experiences. This means more than just tinkering around the edges of what schools currently do. It means that educators must rethink the experiences that students receive all up and down the education system in order to provide kids with deeper knowledge and critical thinking skills that their counterparts in other high-performing First World countries more regularly receive. Thus, introducing Standards is a learning change for adults as well as students.

The Standards seek to bring about instructional change by catalyzing educators to make two important adjustments to students' experiences. First, they ask educators to focus instruction on fewer topics attended to more deeply in mathematics; and on more complex, content-rich nonfiction, as well as fiction, in English language arts (ELA). Second, in both subjects, the Standards encourage teachers to engage students at higher levels of cognitive demand—asking not just for procedural competency but also for conceptual understanding in mathematics and evidence-grounded argumentation in ELA.

Even more challenging, the teachers and school leaders are being asked to make these adjustments as they carry out their day jobs in the trenches of education, where they are often asked to apply chain-of-command logic to deeply contextualized problems. How should they think about major reform implementation all the while doing the messy and demanding work of organizing students' learning experiences among the often fraught psychological terrain of childhood and adolescence?

This chapter focuses on what it means to implement Standards. It draws on the author's twenty years of experience researching reform utilization and on specific examples from research on Common Core implementation in New York City schools from 2011 to 2013. It contends that how leaders organize the problem of standards implementation for school faculty and district staff will have a great impact on how these people take up the challenge posed by standards-based reform. You will notice that standards implementation is framed here foremost as a leadership challenge, not a classroom teacher challenge, because how leaders cast the learning aspects of the task will have a major bearing on how the reform is taken up.

## WHAT DOES IT MEAN TO "IMPLEMENT" STANDARDS?

The method for enacting any external reform, be it broad or targeted, is to *implement* the reform. But what docs it means to "implement" a reform? In essence, *implementation is the process by which an idea becomes embedded into practice.* Yet this phrase leaves a tremendous amount unstated about the process by which the idea is introduced to practitioners; considered by them; accepted, rejected, or reinterpreted; and ultimately, in whole, part, or rendition, incorporated into their regular way of doing things. Put another way, what is the operating theory by which leaders encourage this process?

To help clarify, consider two prevailing—but very different—theories about implementation: *prescription* and *construction*. Implementing a reform prescriptively means introducing it in a particular and externally specified way through a specified script or routine. The reform comes with a specific procedure that, if followed, confers successful implementation. The theory underlying prescription is that people learn by replicating a process repeatedly until it is embedded into their practice.

By contrast, implementing a reform constructively means asking the targets of reform to engage with what it means to incorporate it into their practice and by contributing their *input and judgment* about how best to fit the reform into their own particular situation. In this case, successful implementation means likely making adjustments to the reform to fit the context. The theory underlying construction is that people learn through the experience of molding an idea into their practice.

Thus, whether by prescription or construction, the problem of standards implementation is *both a teaching and learning problem for adults*. As we shall see, the application of these two approaches has important consequences for both leaders and implementers.

Both of these approaches to implementation have trade-offs and an appropriate time and place. Furthermore, successful implementation depends on key aspects of the reform itself as well as the beliefs and capabilities of both leaders and implementers. Some reforms are very well specified and address very particular problems, while other reforms are large ideas that have less clarity about what they will look like in practice. It is tempting at this point to make a distinction between *programs* and *policies*, attributing programs with a need for prescriptive compliance and policies with constructive engagement due to their relative lack of specificity. But that's not quite right, because there are some very prescriptive policies that require compliance and some ambitious programs that demand high levels of local flexibility and judgment.

To add another wrinkle, one might also think of some reforms as consisting of nested layers, with some components asking for prescription and other aspects requiring more flexible construction of solutions. To think in this way challenges the leaders who are designing implementation strategies and guidance to keep both approaches simultaneously in their heads as they develop plans and explanations that ask those in their charge to start using reform ideas in their classrooms.

The rest of this chapter takes the leaders' perspective—at whatever level of the system—as they design implementation policies, routines, activities, and other learning opportunities. Developing implementation strategies as prescription or construction requires leaders to ask four essential questions about the reform, or the component of the reform, that they are asking schools and teachers to implement. Each of these essential questions has important corollary implications and assumptions that are important for leaders to understand.

# QUESTION 1: DOES THE TASK TO BE IMPLEMENTED HAVE A KNOWN SOLUTION?

One important clue about how to think about implementation concerns the nature of the task itself: Does the problem you want to address have a known solution? Ronald Heifetz of Harvard's Kennedy School of Government makes a useful distinction between two very different types of problems that leaders face: *technical problems* and *adaptive challenges* (Heifetz & Linsky, 2002). Technical problems are those for which there are known solutions, however complex they may be, and the task of those faced with a technical challenge is to adopt an already puzzled out solution. Adaptive challenges are more difficult in the sense that they have no readily known solution and therefore cannot just be introduced in a predictable sequence to achieve a desired result.

Thus, the type of challenge posed by the reform represents an important distinction for both leaders and implementers. *We follow procedures to implement solutions to technical challenges, and we engage with adaptive challenges to discover solutions that work in particular situations.* Technical challenges ask for a particular and sequential response. Adaptive challenges require constructive approaches, as school faculties *engage* with the challenge and develop their own best ways that fit their capacity and context.

Should school leaders consider the task of implementing the Common Core to be a technical challenge or an adaptive challenge? The Standards themselves are a set of goals and expectations rather than a well-developed set of instructional approaches, and therefore they leave large latitude about how they should be achieved. To make major adjustments to the content teachers teach and the rigor by which they teach it is uncharted territory for classroom instructors *and* for school and district leaders to support. This points to the overall adaptive nature of the standards implementation challenge, but this does not mean that elements of Standards adoption cannot be broken into prescriptive tasks.

The key point is *to align the implementation approach with the nature of the task*. This alignment was found to be essential in the Consortium for Policy Research in Education's examination of Common Core implementation in New York City from 2011 to 2013 (Goldsworthy, Supovitz & Riggan, 2013). To engage schools with the adaptive challenge of Standards implementation (more on district design later) NYC district leaders crafted a set of activities for schools to deepen their engagement with the Standards. These activities included identifying (or developing) and administering a performance task embedded within a standards-aligned instructional unit and examining the resulting student work in grade groups to identify implications for both curriculum and instruction.

Some schools procedurally fulfilled the district's request by identifying and administering tasks that were largely disconnected from their curriculum or identifying existing assessments that did little to reveal the ways in which the new Standards were different from previous versions. These schools tended to fit the new requests into their existing procedures, and many falsely concluded that they were pretty much already doing what needed to be done because they were following the letter of the district's request.

Other schools took the opportunity to engage more deeply with the suggested district activities and used these experiences as catalysts to explore the ways that the Standards were asking for fundamentally different instructional experiences. They created performance tasks that reflected the rigor of the Standards, and they used the resulting student performance data to collaboratively inquire about both the connections between the Standards and their curriculum, and to reflect on the extent to which their instructional moves facilitated their students' understanding. They reported that these experiences allowed them to deepen their shared understanding of the implications of the Standards for curriculum, instruction, and assessment.

The different experiences of these schools suggest that the nature of leaders' expectations when they introduce reform, coupled with how teachers frame their responses, contribute the depth of learning and level of reform adoption.

## QUESTION 2: HOW IMPORTANT IS FIDELITY TO IMPLEMENTATION?

A second critical consideration of whether to approach implementation prescriptively or constructively is to understand the advantages and disadvantages of *fidelity of implementation*. At first glance, it might seem obvious that leaders want fidelity and the lack of it is due to misunderstanding, indolence, or even resistance. But fidelity assumes two important things. First, fidelity requires that teachers have a clear idea of what to be faithful to, which, as described above, is not always the case. Second, fidelity assumes that a preconceived approach fits all circumstances. But what if faithfulness results in a misapplication of action? Fidelity may also reduce the sense of ownership that comes with making reform one's own.

The pros and cons of fidelity are encapsulated in a long-running debate in educational research circles about its importance to reform implementation success. In these debates, fidelity generally means following a prescriptive process. Advocates of fidelity argue that a reform *must be well specified* and that faithful execution is essential in order for it to be enacted as designed and replicated from site to site (Mills & Ragan, 2000). On the other hand, researchers who have studied how large-scale reforms have been more successfully implemented point to the importance of a process of "mutual adaptation" by which adjustments at both the central and local levels result in modifications to the reform design as they are tailored to fit more snugly into local contexts (McLaughlin, 1987). In this view, implementation is more likely to involve a series of "iterative adaptations" at different levels of the system as implementers adjust the original reform ideas based on their knowledge and prior experience, as well as their particular organizational contexts and resources (Supovitz, 2008).

The takeaways from this research are twofold. First, the relative importance of fidelity hinges on *the specificity of the thing to be implemented.* For example, there are certain components of the Standards, like focusing instructional time on the major mathematics topics at a grade level and following the prescribed sequence of mathematics topics, that may benefit from procedural adoption. Nobody wants fifth-grade teachers teaching second-grade Standards. By contrast, there are other elements of the Standards, like identifying appropriate activities in literacy to build students' content knowledge on a subject or topic, or identifying which mathematics practice to incorporate into a particular lesson, that require teachers to have latitude to choose texts and activities.

The second takeaway is that straying from fidelity depends on *the knowledge level of the implementer to make the right adjustments.* When starting out, fidelity is generally advantageous because those who understand the problem best are those who designed the protocol to be followed. Additionally, the protocol gives learners a process to follow to understand how the reform idea is *intended* to work in practice. But as implementers gain more knowledge of the reform, they should begin to understand how fidelity is contributing to or constraining their optimization.

Thus, fidelity has its limits. Particularly with complex reforms (as most instructional change initiatives are, especially those that press for more cognitively demanding learning) there are inevitably situations where following the procedure does not work because a generic, predesigned protocol cannot account for all circumstances. The paradox is that implementers need to know what they can only learn with experience: which adaptations strengthen the spirit of the reform and which adjustments weaken it. Without substantial knowledge of the reform, implementers are as likely as not to hold on to superficial reform aspects while casting off the essential ideas. And thus we get a repeat of the pattern described at the beginning of this chapter: As reforms spread wider, the form is retained while the core instructional reform ideas grow fainter.

This is where leadership can fill the breach. The role of leaders supporting reform adoption is at least fourfold. First, leaders need to set aside their personal beliefs about the extent to which they value prescription vis-à-vis construction and instead base their expectations for fidelity and their designs for inducing implementation *on the nature of the task to be accomplished.*

Second, leaders must know enough about a reform—or have access to that knowledge—to know what circumstances call for prescription and what situations call for construction. When considering adjustments, the key question is whether the modifications maintain or weaken the core principles that the reform seeks to introduce.

Third, leaders must recognize the psychological implications of whatever strategy they choose. Some school faculties and individual members may be skeptical about the possibility of the Standards to bring about productive change or may be of the "just tell me what to do and I will do it" mindset. Should these beliefs change the calculus of leaders as to whether to infuse implementation requirements with prescriptive or constructive expectations? In such circumstances where leaders see signs of skepticism or resistance, they may want to begin with prescriptive implementation that initially influences practices, with the intent that changes in beliefs will follow (Guskey, 1986).

Finally, leaders should recognize the consequences of relying *solely* on prescriptive reform introduction strategies, because these approaches may reduce faculty members' sense of *ownership* of reform. Adopting a prescriptive approach to reform involves taking up something *external* to oneself that one has very little control over, while constructive implementation asks adopting agents to take *ownership* of reform as they *engage* with its implications for their particular contexts. *Engagement brings with it more ownership, and ownership deepens implementation.*

## QUESTION 3: WHAT KINDS OF LEARNING EXPERIENCES DOES IMPLEMENTATION ASK FOR?

The third question leaders must consider as they think strategically about implementing the Standards is *what* kinds of learning experiences they should provide so that teachers modify their instructional experiences in order for students to learn more. In this way, Standards implementation is a teaching and learning task at all levels of the system: for leaders, teachers, and students. Yet prescriptive and constructive approaches carry with them very different conceptions of what it means to "learn" to introduce a reform.

Prescriptive implementation asks for a more *behavioral learning approach*, whereby adopters are given a set of procedures that they are asked to follow in order to utilize the reform. Faithful introduction comes from following the externally provided approach and enacting a set of practices in a prescribed order. Behaviorist theory is little concerned with cognition but rather relies on replicable routines that alter practice through consistent application. Prescriptive programs typically have a checklist of behaviors that can be observed to see if the practices are being implemented.

By contrast, viewing implementation as construction implies creating—either individually or collectively—the meaning of a reform for one's own context. This implies an underlying constructivist learning approach. Constructivist learning theory *encourages* implementing agents to grapple with how a reform fits into their own environments, to mold the reform to best fit with their own routines, and in doing so to integrate the key elements of the current reform into their practice.

*The lesson here is that how leaders craft the learning experiences of reform will have a major influence on how the reform is received and how schools and teachers approach implementation.* This lesson has major implications for how leaders set up the activities and learning experiences that they use to encourage school faculties to implement a reform. Constructing meaningful activities to promote high levels of cognitive engagement from teachers requires careful attention to policy design.

A good example of how leaders used constructivist learning theory to craft learning experiences for schools is the earlier introduced story of how New York City district leaders developed a parsimonious set of powerful activities intended to catalyze teachers and school leaders to engage with the deep instructional implications of the standards. [1]

The 2011/12 Citywide Instructional Expectations (CIEs) consisted of two fairly straightforward activities. First, the CIEs asked teachers to conduct a gap analysis between the expectations of the Standards and current student capability as manifested in student work. Second, the CIEs asked that all students experience two performance tasks, one in mathematics and one in ELA, embedded within a standards-aligned instructional unit; and that teachers examine the resulting student work in grade groups to identify implications for both curriculum and instruction. These activities were carefully planned to collectively engage teachers in important substantive discussions about their practice. The emphasis on the performance task as a way of revealing representations of student work centered the conversation on the learning outcomes of students rather than the instructional inputs of teachers, and therefore placed the emphasis on what students receive rather than what teachers deliver.

Despite the brevity of the CIEs, they were designed such that educators had to engage with the range of elements that go into effective instruction, including understanding of standards, curriculum, pedagogical strategies, content knowledge, and assessment practices. In this way, the district leaders increased the likelihood of deepening teachers' understanding of the implications of the Standards.

## QUESTION 4: WHERE DOES THE KNOWLEDGE
## FOR IMPLEMENTATION COME FROM?

The fourth question that leaders should ask themselves before designing implementation activities is where the expertise to support reform adoption will come from. Some changes require very different skills or technologies than school faculties currently possess and so must be introduced externally. In other cases, the current skill level of teachers is inadequate for the task. In still other situations, a faculty may have the capacity to implement a change but lack the catalyst for making the adjustment in practice. Finally, as in the case of adaptive challenges, the expertise may simply not be readily available.

The task for leaders is to *identify the locus of expertise for reform implementation*. They should recognize that prescriptive approaches to implementation imply *that the expertise to reach the objective exists, but that it resides outside of the implementing schools*. As Robert Evans noted in his insightful analysis of the psychological effects of school change, this raises teachers' defensiveness because their current way of practice, which represents their faithful best, is implicitly being labeled as inadequate (Evans, 1996). The learning experiences for prescriptive implementation usually involve external experts providing (often off-site) professional development to implementing agents, who are then asked to go back and apply what they have learned to their teaching. While there is often a role for such activities, external training for complex reforms rarely results in deep-rooted change without addressing the underlying reasons that require new practices and allowing for a more contextualized way for learners to iteratively try-discuss-modify-retry the new techniques.

An additional unfortunate tendency of educational leaders is to underestimate the capacity that exists within schools to support reform. In a study of eight New York City schools in 2013 (Supovitz, Fink, & Newman, 2014), one in fourteen faculty members (about 7 percent) were very knowledgeable about either the Common Core in mathematics and English language arts (but even more rarely, both). These individuals tended to be predominantly formal school leaders and coaches, but also teachers. Further, researchers found no overall relationship between individuals' Common Core knowledge and the extent to which their colleagues tapped them for Common Core assistance, although the likelihood was stronger in mathematics than English language arts. This points to both the underutilization of expertise within schools and the differences across subject matter (see Spillane & Hopkins, chapter 4, this volume). One implication of this is that leaders underutilize an important internal resource in schools, which could be identified, positioned, and encouraged to lead and/or support change.

## CONCLUSION

Implementation of the Common Core Standards represents a major challenge for educational leaders. Implementation is the deceptively complex process by which a new idea becomes embedded into regular practice. Current practices are what they are due to a host of prior experiences, including prior efforts to integrate reforms, shaped by both individual and organizational interactions that have solidified over time into the prevailing way of doing things. This is not to say that practices are petrified; but they are generally stable and routinized, with shifts occurring as much unconsciously as consciously.

Reforms enter into this picture, usually championed by external agents who seek to change the prevailing practice by argument or by fiat. Understanding this scenario, it is not surprising that many promising reforms founder on the shoals of mis-implementation. Successful adoption requires skillful leadership to navigate reform ideas into the minds and behaviors of those in their charge.

This chapter has provided leaders with two ways to think about implementation: prescription and construction, each involving very different approaches and implications. Infusing the Common Core Standards into practice will require elements of both implementation approaches. Choosing wisely between them requires leaders to understand the nature of the task to be implemented, the trade-offs of fidelity versus latitude, the learning theories underlying the two approaches, and how to think of the locus of expertise for implementation. Leading the steady and persistent engagement of educators with the meaning of the Standards and their implications for the experiences of students will determine whether we hold tight to the powerful instructional ideas at the core of the Standards that just might make this era of education reform different from those of the past.

## NOTES

1. See Supovitz, Fink, & Newman (2014) for a detailed description of the NYC policy design.

*Chapter Two*

# The Infrastructure and Conceptual Challenges of the Common Core State Standards

*English Language Arts as a Case*

Carol D. Lee

The Common Core State Standards (CCSS) represent a relatively new vision for standards in American education. The politics of its evolution are well documented in other essays in this volume. This chapter takes a different approach, examining tensions between what is already well-known about learning processes, on the one hand, and how this knowledge makes its way—or, just as importantly, *does not* make its way—into the CCSS and the infrastructure meant to support them. To illustrate these tensions, this chapter focuses on the domain of reading across the curriculum in high school, represented in the Common Core State Standards for English Language Arts and Literacy in History/Social Science and Technical Subjects. The goal is to understand what the standards address and what they don't address, as well as the implications of adopting these standards in terms of schools having the capacity, disposition, and resources to fill in the gaps. A third, but closely related, goal is to raise questions about the politics entailed in the uptake of basic research in the design and implementation of public policy in education.

While past efforts at developing rigorous academic standards have not had the national scope of the CCSS, the New Standards Project and the American Diploma Project share with CCSS an attempt to articulate academic standards that move beyond rote learning to address the complex demands of critical thinking and problem solving. Within disciplines, the National

Council of Teachers of Mathematics standards and the several generations of science standards, culminating most recently in the Next Generation Science Standards (NGSS), represent another set of exemplars of using rigorous standards to improve the quality of instruction in U.S. schools.

All of these past efforts share a common fate: the inability of the infrastructure of districts, schools, classrooms, and individual teachers to address the unequal learning opportunities historically associated with students who live in poverty, who are members of historically disenfranchised minority groups, whose first language is other than English, and who may have a history of low academic achievement as represented by scores on an array of standardized and diagnostic tests most typically used in U.S. schools. Many factors contribute to the challenge of scalability with regard to the implementation of such standards. This chapter, however, zooms in on the conceptual issues around learning in disciplines that practitioners on the ground must address, some of which may not be articulated in the standards themselves.

This historic inability to address the rigorous demands requiring critical thinking and problem solving is characterized by a number of "lacks" in the roll out of such standards. Specifically, then and now, the standards do not address the following important factors:

- The lack of a coherent infrastructure for capacity building. Such infrastructure includes teacher preparation, working conditions to support learning in organizations, and specialized in-school supports for teacher learning.
- The lack of any attention to social and emotional demands, which includes identity processes, of the rigorous learning required by the CCSS. This applies to students and teachers alike.
- The lack of pedagogical practices that socialize epistemological orientations and habits of mind required for complex problem solving (e.g., orientations toward issues like wrestling with complexity and ambiguity in how learners approach problems of learning)
- The lack of pedagogical practices that focus on multiple and adaptive pathways through which such learning can be supported, especially for learners with diverse needs
- The lack of a library of tested examples of what such instruction can look like. This might include video cases, samples of student work, or exemplars of generative instructional tasks.[1]

## WHAT TEACHERS NEED TO KNOW TO IMPLEMENT
## THE STANDARDS

Lee Shulman, noted for his articulation of pedagogical content knowledge (e.g., understanding what makes learning difficult for novices), and Deborah Ball, noted for her research on mathematical learning, among others, have talked about the need for teachers and curriculum designers to understand what makes developing rich conceptual understanding difficult for novices. For example, Deborah Ball discovered that her pedagogical content knowledge of the mathematics to be taught in the primary grades was qualitatively different from that of experienced mathematicians. The mathematics she needed to understand about young children learning about fractions was qualitatively different from the formal knowledge of the professional mathematician. In addition to teachers needing to understand what novices need to know in learning academic content, it is equally important that teachers understand sources of resistance and sources of vulnerabilities and strengths that students may have that can contribute to or constrain the students' learning and, in so doing, to understand the multiple pathways through which instruction can be designed to mitigate sources of vulnerability, such as poverty and a history of ineffective teachers. These challenges often require individual teachers, as well as entire schools, to resist stereotypes that lead to a culture of low expectations. Practices entailed in such cultures include tracking that positions low-achieving students so that they are never asked to wrestle with complex learning tasks and low-level instruction focused on rote learning.

## INFRASTRUCTURE NEEDED TO SUPPORT TEACHERS
## IN IMPLEMENTING THE CCSS

From a systems point of view, sometimes these large-scale reform efforts suffer, in part, because there are not sufficient resources available to schools and teachers to meet the demands of the standards. One interesting example is the Reading First initiative to improve reading instruction in the primary grades. On the positive side, there was significant investment in the development of diagnostic tools that schools could use to measure discrete skills in decoding, as well as focused and relatively coherent professional development resources to help teachers and schools generate data that was sufficiently detailed to inform instructional decisions. Interestingly, when the Department of Education tested the long-term impact of Reading First, they found substantive growth in decoding, but virtually no growth in comprehension. This example illustrates how what is *not* addressed in the goals of the reform reasonably inhibits the outcomes. If the Reading First initiative had addressed both decoding and comprehension, and had developed a parallel set of instructional and diagnostic supports for comprehension, would the outcomes have been different?

By contrast, in terms of the English Language Arts (ELA) CCSS standards for middle and high school, few resources are available to teachers and schools for diagnosing strengths and weaknesses in reading across the content areas or the writing of arguments, which are both broad goals that are central to the standards in ELA. And while the assessments that are being developed (Partnership for the Assessment of Readiness for College and Careers [PARCC] and Smarter Balance) may be useful for summative evaluations, they will not provide data on how students are going about tackling the problems of disciplinary texts—diagnostic information that would be extremely useful for informing instruction. In addition, the assessments are not designed to provide teachers with information on the factors that might influence students' abilities to critically comprehend these texts. Such factors include lack of relevant prior knowledge, lack of understanding essential vocabulary, lack of understanding of discipline-specific text structures, and lack of understanding how to reason from evidence to claims in ways that characterize thinking in the disciplines. In addition, while Reading First did lead to state and district efforts to create infrastructure in the form of reading coaches to support teachers, the use of such coaches was largely concentrated in the primary grades. To support teacher learning about how to teach complex comprehension of texts in the disciplines, reading coaches will require a very different kind of knowledge base than most generic reading coaches possess. For example, coaching to support the ELA CCSS goals of critical reading in the disciplines and argumentation requires:

- Deep disciplinary content knowledge, including knowing what is entailed in comprehending texts in history, science, literature, and mathematics.
- Reading-strategy knowledge that is discipline-specific. In history, for example, this includes sourcing, corroboration, contextualization, and the ability to understand differences in text genres that go beyond the distinction between primary and secondary sources.
- Epistemological orientations toward argumentation in disciplines, including viewing literary texts as open to dialogue and viewing history as constructed and contested.
- Pedagogical strategies for supporting problem solving and scaffolding.
- Knowledge of adolescent development in order to understand sources of student resistance and motivation.
- An understanding of adult development for working productively with teachers as learners.

This list represents the challenging array of knowledge required to help teachers learn to engage in rich, discipline-specific reading and composition instruction. And yet programs for teacher preparation, reading specialist certification, and teacher leadership do not routinely provide specialists with these skills.

## POLITICAL CONTEXTS INFLUENCING THE ARTICULATION OF THE STANDARDS

There is another set of interesting links between Reading First and the CCSS in ELA. The decision to focus on decoding in the primary grades was not due to a lack of a sufficient research on early comprehension. The so-called reading wars of the 1990s were more ideological than scientific; and the decision to highlight decoding over comprehension in the Reading First investments was not based on what was known about processes of comprehension. One lesson, then, for reform efforts in K–12 schooling is to understand not only what such standards or initiatives demand that is useful, but also what they leave out that must be addressed if students are to learn to engage in the fullness of the rigorous goals.

These tensions are most often rooted in politics, understanding who are the key players driving policy decisions. These players include politicians, nongovernmental organizations, foundations, professional unions, and business people. Researchers represent another important group of players; they are often invited to participate because they represent an orientation that other vested interests hold. While the CCSS called for an open process of deliberating the standards among an array of vested interest groups, the emerging backlash confronting the CCSS suggests that some communities have felt left out of the process. Adding to the complexity, neither the processes of inclusiveness nor the evolving backlash are deeply informed by the full array of available research on reading comprehension, reading in the disciplines, argumentation, or composition.

## TENSIONS WITHIN BASIC RESEARCH AND ITS UPTAKE IN THE STANDARDS

The CCSS project made explicit efforts to connect the standards to existing research. For example, appendix A of the ELA standards describes the research base underlying how the standards address problems like understanding sources of text complexity. The CCSS in ELA call for students to learn to read complex texts at earlier grades, to read widely in all content areas, and to be able to construct arguments around generative questions in the content areas by close reading and critical examination of texts. There is no question that these are laudatory goals, and ones that will be necessary to prepare students for college and career readiness. Though such standards were embedded in the College Readiness Standards (CRS) articulated by the College Board, there were so many standards that it was challenging to translate them into instructional goals that were manageable. Developers of the CCSS made a conscious decision, starting with outcome goals for twelfth grade, to focus on a smaller and more coherent articulation of goals: more complex texts; close reading; reading across the curriculum; argumentation. Research on the design of academic standards has wrestled with questions around how detailed standards need to be in order to be useful for practitioners. For example, at one point, the National Council of Teachers of English created ELA standards that were one page in length. In addition, research in mathematics education has emphasized teaching fewer topics in depth.

However, in the efforts to then backtrack from twelfth grade to articulate grade-level standards for these four broad goals, they came up against at least two challenges: (a) how to define text complexity; and (b) how to create a developmental progression across the grades. The grade-level progressions suffer from a long-standing tradition in the articulation of ELA goals: reading comprehension standards (whether at the state level, in College Readiness Standards or National Assessment of Educational Progress [NAEP] reading framework) typically repeat the same skills from one grade level or grade band to another with minor and quite arbitrary differences in wording to suggest that the skill is becoming more complex.

This problem is not only a historical one concerning how grade-level standards in reading comprehension have been articulated in the past, but equally a scientific conundrum in the field of reading. The conundrum is that most measures of text complexity—that is, how to figure out whether a group of third or fifth or eighth or eleventh graders should be able to read a particular text with understanding—focus only on the surface features of texts, such as length, sentence syntax, or vocabulary. These are the dimensions of text complexity in most readability formulas that teachers are familiar with and have easy access to. Such dimensions are also used in the Lexile framework, a measure that assigns difficulty levels associated with grade bands and that has a very usable website where teachers can look up common texts to see their readability. There are newer tools available to text complexity quantitatively and automatically (examples include Coh-Metrix, which analyzes sources of coherence in texts and how they might contribute to readability, and TextEvaluator, which examines more nuanced features of vocabulary, syntax, narrative style, and argumentation structure). But these newer tools are not readily available to practitioners and on the whole require a high degree of technical knowledge to use them effectively.

This limited focus on how to figure out the readability of particular texts for particular groups of students poses several problems. First, a text can have simple words and short sentences and still be very difficult to comprehend. For example, in literature a brief story written with simple language might engage with complex themes and characters. And so even though average readers are able to say the words on the page, they might not be able to access these words' deeper, figurative meanings. Similarly, in each of the content areas—literature, history, science, and mathematics—the organization of the text, rather than the simplicity of the vocabulary or sentences, can make comprehension challenging.

Second, comprehension difficulty is associated not only with the nature of the text but also with the nature of the task. You can have what appears to be a simple text in terms of length and language, but the task associated with it might be challenging. For example, in history, the standards (not only the CCSS but also in the history standards within the discipline) call for readers to wrestle with understanding the historical context in which the text was produced, to interrogate what may be any biases of the author, and to corroborate claims in the text against the historical record. In addition, history comprehension standards included in the ELA CCSS ask students to wrestle with these problems of historical reasoning across multiple texts. In the teaching of history, these are called document-based questions, in which students interrogate a complex historical question by reading multiple texts. What is emerging in the field of reading comprehension, especially reading in the content areas, is articulating the problem of comprehension difficulty as situated in relationships between texts and tasks. For example, a text can be short and use simple language, as with Alice Walker's short story "The Flowers." But if the task is to interpret the symbolism in the story rather than recall the literal plot, then the complexity of what students have to do is centered neither in the text alone nor in the task alone, but in how features of the text (in this case simple descriptive language that can be read as both literal and figurative) intersect with the complexity or simplicity of the task students are asked to engage. This relationship is further complicated by studies that argue for the importance of context to encompass text-task-context as interrelated sources of complexity in comprehension. For example, how do we account for the observation that we have students who struggle to read with understanding in school, but who engage in complex reading and argumentation in informal learning environments outside of school? This phenomenon suggests that students' abilities to read critically can be influenced by the contexts in which they engage in reading. In community-based learning environments (playing digital games, using digital media to examine societal issues in a Boys and Girls Club or Digital Youth Media organization), learners often have greater intrinsic motivation to engage the task—in this case of reading—and greater supports from peers and others to become competent. These everyday learning environments are often more pedagogically engaging than schools.

The point here is that there is a strong research base in support of the idea that complexity of comprehension grows out of the nature of the complexity in the text(s), the tasks, and the contexts in which learning to wrestle with texts takes place. The problem in implementing the ELA CCSS to achieve the desired outcomes equitably is that the standards do not address these issues. The standards point to quantitative tools for assessing text complexity (such as Lexiles and traditional text-difficulty measures) and some very general qualitative guidelines for teachers to use. However, these tools are not sufficient for making well-informed decisions about text selections. The standards offer exemplary lists of texts by content areas and grade levels without providing any rationale for why these texts were chosen. The choices not only appear to be totally arbitrary, but in some cases the choices raise questions about whether they are developmentally appropriate for particular groups of students.

These challenges concerning text complexity and text selection are essential conundrums to be wrestled with if the desired goals of the standards for reading comprehension are to be met. These are in addition to the infrastructure challenges regarding diagnostic tools, rigorous curriculum materials, exemplary cases of robust instruction, professional development opportunities, and so forth. How can schools and districts organize themselves as learning organizations to tackle a problem that is essential to the enterprise but which the standards—as well as much of the industry that is evolving to support their implementation—do not address? This challenge is at the heart of what it means to teach.

Despite the availability of standards, well-crafted curriculum, scripted curriculum, required reading lists, learning is not a transmission model. Children and adolescents are not empty vessels into which teachers can pour information, knowledge, and dispositions. Rather, as in all human relationships, learning is about relationship building, about wrestling to understand the internal state, goals, aspirations, resources, and vulnerabilities of the other. That means we are always interacting with other people as we engage in complex problem solving around tasks that are ill structured and for which there is no single right pathway. To what extent, and in what ways, are schools as learning organizations situated to support all stakeholders (administrators, teachers, staff, students, parents) in understanding what we, as a society, are trying to achieve? How are schools able to test multiple pathways for achieving these goals?

Professionally, such problem solving requires deep disciplinary knowledge in several domains: conceptual understanding of how people learn; multiple pathways through which engagement, motivation, and grit develop; basic classroom management; relationships between sources of risk and sources of resilience; how participation in multiple contexts (family, peer social networks, informal learning environments outside of school, neighborhood resources) provides resources for identity building; goal setting; and engagement. Such professional problem solving also requires wrestling with what are often implicit biases deriving from negative stereotypes that can trigger low expectations, hide the ability to construe sources of resilience in the face of extreme risk, and constrain how learning opportunities are structured. This is a historic challenge that every reform effort has had to face, generally with little success. It involves a set of conversations in the public and within the profession that we examine typically very superficially.

Bottom line: Teaching is hard, even for the best teachers. Because of the complexity of teaching, the profession requires what some call *adaptive expertise*—the ability to adapt foundational knowledge to unexpected circumstances. Reading comprehension and argumentation always involve unexpected circumstances, by the very nature of texts and the multiple resources people have for engaging meaningfully with texts. Because of this complexity, any attempt at large-scale reforms, especially on a national level in a federal democratic system that decentralizes education, will require an infrastructure that supports knowledge production as the core practice of teaching.

## NOTES

1. While the New Standards Project did provide examples of exemplary student work, there was not a sufficient publicly supported system of distribution to have a large-scale impact, and the exemplars did not address how such tasks would be accomplished with important subgroups of students, such as students for whom English is a second language or students who are academically struggling.

## Chapter Three

# Implementing the Common Core

*How Individuals, Organizational Resources, and Instructional Practice Matter*

## John B. Diamond

The Common Core State Standards (CCSS) are the latest standards-based reform designed to create more educational equity by creating rigorous standards and linking them to better assessments. Proponents argue that this reform will better prepare students for college and twenty-first-century jobs. The logic behind these reforms is relatively straightforward. Clear standards will clarify what students should know and be able to do at each grade level throughout the education system. With the development of these common standards, teachers and educational leaders will be able to develop practices that help all students reach higher levels of achievement. In order to monitor student learning and hold schools accountable, states are expected to adopt assessments that are aligned to the CCSS.

This approach is rooted in the assumption that mandates handed down through government agencies strongly shape practices at the district, school, and classroom levels. But decades of educational reform efforts have demonstrated that such links among policy, administrative leadership, and instructional practice are more complicated than this model would suggest (Cuban, 2013). Rather than a direct link between standards, accountability, and classroom practice, the ways that standards influence instruction are complicated and involve multiple mediating factors.

This chapter highlights three research findings about policy implementation that have clear implications for reform efforts related to the CCSS. These findings can be summed up in three statements:

- How policies are implemented depends on how people make sense of them.
- How policies play out depends on school-level organizational resources and capacity.
- How policies connect to instruction depends on instructional dimension and subject area.

   The rest of this chapter describes each of these findings and their implications for how school and district leaders might approach the implementation of the CCSS.

## HOW POLICIES ARE IMPLEMENTED DEPENDS ON HOW PEOPLE MAKE SENSE OF THEM

When policymakers draft legislation they are sending messages to schools that they hope will lead to responses that yield the desired outcomes. The CCSS, for example, emphasize creating more rigorous learning environments throughout students' educational trajectories that will prepare them for college and career more effectively than they currently do. By creating standards at each grade level in mathematics and language arts, and assessing students' progress, policymakers expect that schools and districts will change their practices in ways that will lead to improved student outcomes. But once policy messages leave the page, they must be interpreted and enacted at the school and district levels. Work on sense-making provides some insight into how this happens (Weick, 1979).

   In the context of educational reform efforts, sense-making is the process through which educational policies are interpreted, responded to, and shaped by those charged with implementing them. Previous research shows that this process is influenced by people's prior beliefs about instruction, their past professional experiences, how school and district leaders define the reforms, and the makeup of teachers' and leaders' social networks (Coburn, 2004; Spillane, 2004). These processes, among many others, can shape how policies play out in practice.

   In the case of the CCSS (and really any reform) sense-making plays a particularly prominent role. That is because while standards are explicit regarding desired outcomes, the people implementing the policy must determine how to reach those outcomes. All of the materials associated with the standards—from the standards themselves to the myriad curricular materials that claim to be CCSS aligned—must be made sense of and incorporated into practice. This is a complex process to say the least. It involves individuals and groups of people who together must determine what is being communicated about instructional practice, and what course of action to take based on those interpretations.

## SENSE-MAKING AND CLASSROOM PRACTICE

One way to think about sense-making is to examine how policy messages influence instructional practice. A particularly informative study conducted by Cynthia Coburn (2004) took this approach by carefully documenting how English teachers in California responded to changing messages about language arts instruction between 1983 and 1999. Coburn examined three teachers' responses to 223 policy messages—the "specific statements or exhortations about how teachers *should* or *must* teach reading" (Coburn, 2004: 217)—over this period and categorized these responses (see figure 3.1). Coburn identified changes in policy messages about literacy instruction from basic skills instruction to balanced instruction. Beginning in the 1980s, there was a push for literature-based instruction that challenged the dominant paradigm of basic skills instruction that had held sway since the 1960s. By the mid-1990s policy messages once again shifted, this time calling for balanced instruction, which emphasized a middle ground between basic skills and literature-based instruction. Coburn identified five types of responses to these policy shifts on the part of teachers.

- **Rejection**: teachers dismissed an approach altogether.
- **Decoupling**: teachers responded symbolically but not substantively.
- **Parallel structures**: when faced with competing policy messages, teachers created two or more structures to respond to the competing messages.
- **Assimilation**: teachers interpreted the policy messages in ways that transformed the messages to fit with their prior beliefs and practices.
- **Accommodation**: teachers engaged with the policy message in ways that changed their fundamental beliefs and practices.

As can be seen from figure 3.1, teachers' most common response to the policy messages was assimilation (49 percent), meaning that teachers interpreted the messages through the lens of their prior practices, thus fundamentally transforming the intent of the policy in practice. In other words, teachers paid attention to the messages but did not fundamentally change their instruction.[1]

The second most common response was rejection (29 percent). Here teachers did not really do anything differently in their classrooms when confronted with the policy message. Decoupling (engaging in symbolic rather than substantive responses) and the creation of parallel structures (adding an additional practice on top of current practice) happened in 7 percent and 8

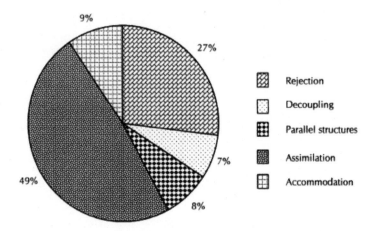

**Figure 3.1.   Teachers' Responses to Policy Messages about Reading, 1983–1999**

percent of cases, respectively. Accommodation, the desired outcome in which teachers fundamentally transformed their practices in line with the intention of the policy message, happened in only 9 percent of cases (where cases equal the 223 policy messages).

It also turned out that there was an interplay between the nature of the messages and how they were interpreted and responded to by these teachers. Policy messages were more likely to influence instructional practice when they were congruent with teachers' prior beliefs, supported through opportunities for professional development and collegial interaction, and engaged in voluntarily by teachers without strong pressure resulting from external sanctions.

This research suggests that educational leaders need to recognize that sense-making is part of the policy implementation process, and that what they view as the appropriate responses to policy messages sent by the CCSS are not self-evident. Instead, the policy messages require deep, substantive engagement with complex ideas in order to be understood and implemented well. Second, simply because a policy message is heard and responded to does not mean it will be enacted in ways that are consistent with the goals of the policy. Third, there are things that can be done to improve the likelihood that policies will be enacted in the spirit in which they were intended. These include helping teachers understand how policies connect, and fail to connect, to their prior belief systems; providing ongoing contexts for meaningful engagement around the standards; and limiting the emphasis on punitive sanctions.

Leaders might try to identify different types of teachers' responses to the CCSS and develop strategies for supporting teachers to make changes. For instance, for teachers who are engaged in assimilating rather than accommodating responses to the CCSS, leaders might use formative evaluations of instruction (conducted by administrators or other teachers) to help make the teachers' prior understandings about instruction explicit and to reflect on the changes needed to respond more fully. Likewise, leaders may identify one set of strategies for teachers who reject the CCSS and another set for those who engage in symbolic response. Finally, district and state leaders might attempt to reduce the perception and reality of punitive accountability sanctions associated with CCSS.

Educational leaders might also reflect on some of the following questions: How do people understand the policy? What opportunities have been provided for substantive conversations about the meaning of the CCSS and how can conclusions reached in these discussions be incorporated into practice? How are members of the school community acting on their understanding of CCSS? How congruent are these actions with the intent of the policy? Are such connections made explicit?

## HOW POLICIES CONNECT TO INSTRUCTION VARIES BY INSTRUCTIONAL DIMENSION AND SUBJECT MATTER

The CCSS are designed to influence instruction, which is sometimes treated as a monolithic, straightforward process of teachers delivering content to students. In reality, teaching and learning are complex activities that involve multiple instructional dimensions and take place across multiple distinct school subject areas. For instance, in a typical classroom, instruction can be thought of as being composed of several related activities, including the following:

- Content coverage
- Teaching strategies (pedagogy)
- Classroom management
- Discipline
- Assessment
- Grouping arrangements
- Selecting instructional materials

Just thinking about the numerous decisions that need to be made moment-to-moment in the typical classroom across these dimensions begins to highlight the complexity of teaching and learning.

Instruction is also deeply rooted in its subject matter in many ways. Differences in content aside, teaching is organized differently in mathematics than it is in language arts, science, and social studies. The subject also influences how school leadership is practiced (see Spillane & Hopkins, chapter 4, this volume; Stodolsky, 1988). Therefore, it is not enough to discuss how the CCSS should influence instruction. Instead, educational leaders need to attend to the complexity of instruction and develop more sophisticated ways of thinking about these connections. Given that instruction is a multifaceted activity that occurs across numerous subject areas, careful reflection is needed regarding how the CCSS will influence specific instructional dimensions within specific subject areas. For instance, school leaders might reflect on how the configuration of teacher leaders varies across mathematics and language arts, and structure interventions accordingly. They might also provide teachers with opportunities to reflect on the implications of the CCSS for specific instructional dimensions.

Just as instruction is not a monolithic activity, the CCSS are not a unitary policy. Rather, multiple related components are associated with this policy. There are the standards themselves, of course, but there are also assessments designed to measure student achievement, textbooks that are supposedly aligned to the Common Core, and tools of various sort that are designed to support implementation of the standards. Those elements may each have an impact on instructional practices, but these impacts may vary across instructional dimensions and subject areas.

For example, in a study of high-stakes accountability reforms in Chicago K–8 schools, Diamond (2007) examined how teachers' instructional practices were influenced by standards-based accountability reforms in that city. He focused on how standards, testing, and textbooks influenced teachers' instructional decisions, demonstrating that all three had a stronger impact on content coverage than on pedagogy (teaching strategies). One major takeaway from this study is that simply because teachers respond to a reform does not mean its influence will be the same across different dimensions of instruction.

This and other work shows that when such policies influence content, they tend to narrow the content covered to that which is tested, lead to fragmented rather than integrated coverage of the subjects taught, lead to some school subject areas getting less attention than others, and encourage teachers to spend inordinate time on test preparation.

Understanding the complexity and multidimensionality of instruction should help educational leaders think more carefully about the potential influence of the CCSS and how as leaders they might support local implementation of the new standards. For instance, in mathematics the CCSS emphasize key shifts from previous standards in how *rigor* is defined. On the CCSS website     (www.corestandards.org/other-resources/key-shifts-in-mathematics/)

*rigor* emphasizes pursuing "conceptual understanding, procedural skills and fluency, and application with equal intensity."[2]

Creating a classroom experience that responds to these shifts requires more than just selecting certain instructional materials (a textbook or mathematics series, for example) or organizing instruction in groups or having students explain their answers. It requires attending to each of the dimensions of instruction in interaction and thinking about how teaching and learning are organized to lead to the desired outcomes. Creating contexts in which these connections can be made explicit and developing mechanisms for ongoing reflection will increase the likelihood of reaching the desired outcomes.

## HOW POLICIES PLAY OUT DEPENDS ON SCHOOL-LEVEL ORGANIZATIONAL RESOURCES AND CAPACITY

The CCSS require a substantial shift in current instructional practices—particularly in schools that have traditionally struggled with standards- and accountability-based reforms. In order for these shifts to be realized, substantial resources and school- and district-based supports are needed. Unfortunately, educational resources are unequally distributed across U.S. schools. Low-income students and students of color are often located in schools and classrooms with the fewest resources (Diamond, 2013).

One way to think about this institutional inequality is to reflect on the current distribution of teachers.[3] While there are some excellent teachers in all schools, the most experienced and highly credentialed teachers teach the most affluent students in the whitest schools. A student of color in a low-income school is anywhere from three to ten times more likely to have a novice teacher, an underprepared teacher, or a teacher working outside his or her discipline than students in majority-white, affluent schools (Adamson & Darling-Hammond, 2012; Darling-Hammond, 2010; Peske & Haycock, 2006). This is particularly disturbing, given strong evidence that teacher qualifications matter for student academic success (Darling-Hammond & Post, 2000).

This creates an important challenge, given current racial and socioeconomic disparities in students' education outcomes. The current distribution of teachers often matches the students from social groups who, on average, struggle the most to meet standards with the teachers least likely equipped to help them meet those standards. In addition to these differences across schools, teacher tracking—the placing of the most experienced and talented teachers in the highest-performing classrooms—across educational levels also creates unequal educational opportunities (Finley, 1984; Kelly, 2004).

We also know that when teachers seek guidance in transforming instructional practices, they turn to their teaching colleagues more than other people in their organizations (Bidwell, 2001; Jackson & Bruegmann, 2009). For example, consistent with prior research on influences on teachers' instructional practices, Diamond (2012) showed that when Chicago teachers were asked about influences on changes in their instructional practices, they relied more on their teaching colleagues and themselves than they did on administrators.

The information that teachers receive (and the usefulness of that information) is therefore shaped by their teaching colleagues. It turns out that schools serving low-income students and students of color tend to emphasize more conventional teaching methods such as recitation, seat work, and lecture (Gamoran, Secada & Marrett, 2000)—just the type of instruction that the CCSS seek to move teachers away from. When teachers are embedded in such schools, they may be less likely to get the support they need from their colleagues. When internal capacity is unequal across schools, standards-based accountability policies may exacerbate, rather than fundamentally challenge, inequality.

Moreover, when schools that have traditionally struggled to reach high levels of student achievement are pressured to make dramatic changes under the threat of sanctions, there may be an increased likelihood of system-gaming responses. Such responses include:

• Using testing data to justify withdrawing resources from the lowest-performing students;
• Targeting resources toward specific grade levels, subject areas, and students that will have a positive impact on a school's accountability status but not on student learning;
• Engaging in symbolic rather than substantive changes in instruction;
• Focusing teaching heavily on tested material.

Capacity building is critical to the successful implementation of the CCSS. Fundamental changes in instructional practices depend on ensuring that the internal capacity in schools does not remain stratified by race, income, and educational track. To address these issues of capacity and equity, leaders should carefully examine hiring practices, the distribution of teachers across schools and classrooms, and the quality of learning opportunities for teachers within and across schools. They might ask some of the following questions: What are the changes needed in specific schools? How are resources allocated to meet those specific needs? How can equality of educational opportunity be maximized?

## CONCLUSION

Those charged with leading the implementation of the CCSS can benefit from three lessons learned from previous standards-based reforms. First, leaders should attend to sense-making processes at the district, school, and classroom levels and provide opportunities for substantive, sustained discussions that help people make sense of the standards and implement them in ways that are consistent with their intentions. Second, leaders can help frame the complexity of the links between the components of the CCSS and the multiple dimensions of instruction across school subjects. By helping school faculty think carefully about the complexity of these links, they can help make implicit ideas about instructional change more explicit and purposeful. Finally, school leaders can help ensure that internal organizational capacity is made more equal and that allocation of instructional resources helps interrupt current patterns of inequality.

## NOTES

1. Coburn's research is based on a small number of teachers. This close analysis of the responses of these teachers over a number of years and over 220 policy messages provides a basis for theoretical rather than statistical generalization. The response categories are designed to help researchers and practitioners reflect on the categories of responses to inform further research and practice but not to suggest that these response percentages would be duplicated in other settings.

2. While proponents of the CCSS discuss these shifts as new, they have similarities with the National Science Foundation mathematics reforms of the 1980s and 1990s.

3. This does not imply that teachers should be blamed for educational inequality. There are major structural challenges related to residential segregation, divestment in urban areas, school funding patterns, social supports for families, and school choice processes that contribute to educational inequalities.

*Chapter Four*

# School-Subject Variation in Educational Infrastructures

*A Cautionary Implementation Tale*

James P. Spillane and Megan Hopkins

Instructional reform—here we go again! Yet another broadscale effort is underway to improve the quality of teaching and learning in American K–12 classrooms, this time taking shape as the Common Core State Standards (CCSS) and the Next Generation Science Standards (NGSS). Although there is debate about how academically rigorous the standards are, especially in science (Gross et al., 2013), there is also reason to celebrate this most recent movement to improve the quality of teaching and learning in American classrooms.

But such improvement will be in great measure a function of the local implementation of CCSS and NGSS, and that will ultimately depend on the efforts of district and school leaders and classroom teachers (Stage et al., 2013). These local efforts will be shaped in important ways by the educational infrastructure that is in place to support classroom instruction and instructional improvement efforts. Educational infrastructures are familiar to anyone who works in the education sector: They are the structures that states, school districts, and schools use to provide instruction and improve it.

This chapter takes a close look at the educational infrastructure for supporting instruction and instructional improvement, revealing how it varies by school subject—and does so in ways that are consequential for CCSS and NGSS implementation. Even more troubling, these subject-matter differences in the educational infrastructure may be accentuated for particular groups of students, such as English language learners, who traditionally have not been well served by the school system and thereby pose unique implementation challenges.

Hence, this cautionary note centers not on the standards themselves, but on their implementation in America's schoolhouses and classrooms, particularly in mathematics and science. If history is any judge, the implementation hurdles for the CCSS, and especially the NGSS, are immense as tens of thousands of American schools take them up, figure them out, and implement them.

## MAPPING EDUCATIONAL INFRASTRUCTURES

Curricular materials, learning standards, student assessments, and teacher instructional guides are the components of educational infrastructure that are probably familiar to most readers, as they are the primary means for guiding instruction. Also under the rubric of educational infrastructure are other, less obvious, components. These include school system and school organizational routines such as grade-level meetings, teacher hiring, and teacher evaluations; formal positions such as mentor teachers, coaches, and literacy coordinators; and tools of various sorts, among them teacher-evaluation rubrics or protocols. Even though these less obvious aspects of the infrastructure are often taken for granted, they are important in that they guide classroom practice, monitor instructional quality, and support teacher learning and, by extension, instructional improvement.

Educational infrastructure has regulative, normative, and cultural-cognitive dimensions. The regulative dimension specifies what school leaders and teachers are required to do; for example, school policy might require that teachers attend weekly grade-level meetings to plan instruction. The normative dimension refers to school norms that value (or do not value) collaboration and the exchange of instructional information among teachers. The cultural-cognitive dimensions include overarching ideas about how to teach and what should be taught, for instance, school leaders' and teachers' beliefs about how to teach mathematics or about how to improve reading instruction. These dimensions can influence school leaders and teachers, work related to instruction including classroom practice and efforts to improve it. Educational infrastructures vary widely among states, schools districts, and even schools within the same local school districts. Some school leaders and teachers work in and with educational infrastructures that clearly and reasonably specify instructional goals and provide support for maintaining and improving the quality of instruction. Others work in and with impoverished educational infrastructures that offer weak and often incoherent guidance about instruction and its improvement. The meaning of CCSS and NGSS for classroom instruction will ultimately be worked out within these distinctly different educational infrastructures, some enabling richer, more focused deliberations, and learning more from and about instruction than others.

Educational infrastructures also vary radically by school subject—*even within the same school and school district*. And this is the challenge that local school leaders and teachers need to acknowledge as they grapple with the CCSS and NGSS. Those intent on using the CCSS and NGSS to improve the quality of teaching in American classrooms would do well to take into account this uneven subject-matter terrain as they face the daunting implementation hurdles ahead.

## HOW THE EDUCATION SYSTEM'S EDUCATIONAL INFRASTRUCTURE DIFFERS BY SCHOOL SUBJECT

When it comes to implementing national educational standards in the United States, *the school subject* is important. Subject-matter differences in the educational infrastructure will significantly determine how much the CCSS and NGSS meaningfully influence the instructional practices experienced by America's youth. These implementation challenges are especially daunting for science, but also potentially for mathematics, because of the state of these subjects' educational infrastructures relative to English language arts (also referred to as "reading" in federal policy). Among the core subjects at the elementary school level, science does not fare well in the local educational infrastructure terrain. Mathematics does better, but not nearly as well as English language arts.

That the educational infrastructure in local school districts and schools differs so dramatically across school subjects is neither a natural nor a social given. Instead, it is a function of past policy design decisions and an accident of history. And the varied terrain is evident at all levels, from Congress to the schoolhouse. At the federal level, the most recent authorization of the Elementary and Secondary Education Act, more commonly known as No Child Left Behind (NCLB), focuses primarily on reading and mathematics, mandating the measurement of school, district, and state progress on achievement tests primarily in those two subjects (National Center for Education Statistics, 2000). Whereas states must measure progress for every child in reading and math in each of grades three through eight and once in grades ten through twelve, science testing is required only once in grades three through five, once in grades six through nine, and once in grades ten through twelve.

Moreover, a school's or district's Adequate Yearly Progress (AYP) is measured only in reading and math. Additionally, funding streams embedded in the legislation under Title I, meant for states to support under-resourced schools, initially only required states to adopt academic standards for all students in language arts and mathematics, with science coming into focus four years after the law's passage.

In alignment with national trends, state-level legislators have long privileged language arts and mathematics over science. By 1999, forty-eight states had articulated standards for language arts and mathematics and adopted accompanying assessments, but only thirty-three states had similar arrangements for elementary school science (Council of Chief State School Officers, 2000). This emphasis on language arts and mathematics was reinforced with NCLB's passage in 2001, with most states continuing to develop or revise standards in language arts and mathematics between 2001 and 2005. In contrast, most states had no science standards prior to NCLB's passage; by 2005 only twenty-seven states had adopted science-content standards and standards-aligned assessments (Editorial Projects in Education Research Center, 2006). Despite policymakers' efforts to level the playing field for all students, science was never foregrounded like other core school subjects.

And there is evidence that these subject-matter differences in the federal and state educational infrastructure, as reflected in accountability policies, may have contributed to decreases in the amount of time devoted to science teaching in elementary schools (Levine, Lopez & Marcelo, 2008; McMurrer, 2007). While districts and schools increased time devoted to tested subjects after NCLB, they reduced time for other subjects, including science (McMurrer, 2007; Morton & Dalton, 2007).

Even more worrying, students enrolled in schools serving large proportions of students of color and economically disadvantaged students may have experienced an especially sharp decline in time spent on science instruction. Specifically, results from the Schools and Staffing Survey indicated that schools with the highest proportions of Black and Latino students and students receiving free and reduced-priced lunches experienced the greatest post-NCLB declines in the instructional time teachers spent on science (National Center for Educational Statistics, 2000). This shift is to be expected, considering that performance incentives for schools are tied to particular populations of students in particular school subjects.

At the same time, these differential incentives play out in schools where the subject-matter terrain for supporting instruction and efforts to improve it are uneven to begin with. Although the greatest decreases in instructional time in the era of accountability were experienced in science, science has always been something of a poor relation to elementary mathematics and language arts. Even before NCLB, elementary teachers devoted much less time to teaching science compared with mathematics and language arts, with about 75 percent of the instructional week devoted to teaching language arts and mathematics compared to just 12 percent devoted to science (Schools and Staffing Survey, 1999–2000).

# HOW SCHOOLS' EDUCATIONAL INFRASTRUCTURE DIFFERS BY SCHOOL SUBJECT

School-subject differences in educational infrastructure exist not just at the system level—they carry over to individual schools as well. To make matters worse, school-level educational infrastructures tend to be more impoverished for mathematics and science than language arts. Language arts has the lion's share of resources, with more elaborate infrastructures to support instruction than mathematics or science (Price & Ball, 1997; Spillane et al., 2001). For example, studies show that organizational routines at the elementary level, including grade-level, curriculum, or leadership meetings, tend to focus on language arts and mathematics, with few routines related to science instruction or its improvement (Hayton & Spillane, 2008; Spillane, 2005).

Additionally, there is some evidence that school norms differ by school subject, with school leaders less likely to choose to be involved in math-related organizational routines that support teacher collaboration than language arts–related routines (Spillane, Parise & Sherer, 2011). Elementary schools also tend to dedicate more formal leadership positions to language arts than any other subject, with leadership positions in mathematics less frequent and positions in science practically nonexistent (Spillane & Hopkins, 2013).

It is common to find school districts with instructional coaches or specialists focused on literacy or language arts assigned to every elementary school building, yet only a few, if any, itinerant mathematics coaches assigned to multiple schools, and no such coaches in science. Given that the presence of an instructional coach is associated with increases in school staff interactions that are indicators of teacher learning and knowledge development, then teachers' opportunities to learn about math instruction—and especially science—are likely impoverished compared to language arts (Spillane & Hopkins, 2013; Hopkins et al., 2013). The implementation of the CCSS and NGSS will thus take place within educational infrastructures for supporting instruction and learning about instruction that differ vastly depending on the school subject.

These school-subject differences in the educational infrastructure do influence day-to-day practice related to instruction in schools. By way of illustration, consider data from fourteen elementary schools in one school district, here called Auburn Park (not its real name), where the social networks for sharing advice and information among school staff members were examined. In those schools, language arts instructional networks were on average 50 percent denser than mathematics networks and 150 percent denser than science networks, meaning that there was more overall advice and information sharing related to language arts relative to math and science (Spillane &

Hopkins, 2013). Further, mathematics networks were 66 percent denser than science networks.

When the educational infrastructure was redesigned in mathematics by, among other things, introducing formal leadership positions for mathematics instruction, the amount of activity centering on sharing math advice and information became much more similar to language arts; science activity, however, remained low and fragmented. Figure 4.1 demonstrates these trends in one of the fourteen schools, showing the nexus of activity centered on instructional coaches in language arts and mathematics, yet a highly fragmented network of instructional advice and information in science.

Considering these differences in the educational infrastructure by school subject, and assuming that similar patterns are common in the United States, the implementation challenges facing this next generation of standards will differ depending on the school subject.

## HOW THE EDUCATIONAL INFRASTRUCTURE DIFFERS BY SCHOOL SUBJECT AND STUDENT POPULATION

Subject-matter differences in the educational infrastructure may also be experienced differently depending on the particular student population under consideration. Take English language learners (ELLs), for example, who will face particular challenges with respect to meeting the learning goals outlined in the CCSS and NGSS, as the standards represent a significant shift in the

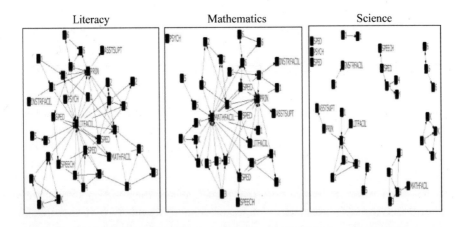

**Figure 4.1.   Chamberlain Elementary School (with mathematics facilitator) social network diagrams by subject, 2012, showing nearly equivalent density and network activity in language arts and mathematics with the addition of instructional coaches in each subject, compared to a low-density, highly fragmented network in science.**

subject-specific language competencies required of students (Bunch, Kibler & Pimentel, 2012; Moschkovich, 2012; Lee, Quinn & Valdes, 2013). Even though ELLs represent over 10 percent of the school-age population and are the fastest-growing student group in the United States (Calderon, Slavin & Sanchez, 2011), the vast majority of general education teachers have had very little, if any, specific training related to teaching ELLs and generally feel unprepared to work with them (Gándara, Maxwell-Jolly & Driscoll, 2005; Zehler et al., 2008).

Because general education teachers lack training and expertise to serve ELLs in the core school subjects, it is critical that district and school leaders design educational infrastructures that enable collaboration between general education teachers and teachers who have specialized training in English as a second language (ESL). In other words, creating educational infrastructures that facilitate interactions between ESL and general education teachers increases the likelihood that general education teachers (such as teachers of English language arts, math, and science) can learn about teaching ELL students and improving ELL instruction in the core school subjects. This is especially true in school districts with large populations of new immigrants, where the predominant response to increasing ELL populations is to implement ESL pull-out programs, which focus on language and literacy development but require ELLs to learn mathematics and science in the general education classroom without additional language supports (Kandel & Parrado, 2006; Lowenhaupt, in press).

A study of one school district with large numbers of new immigrants, here referred to as Twin Rivers, revealed that the infrastructure for supporting ELL instruction looked relatively similar across school subjects at one level. On closer examination, however, substantial differences were evident. Specifically, differences in the normative and cultural-cognitive aspects of the educational infrastructure meant that ESL teachers were used differently depending on the school subject. General education and ESL teachers only interacted with one another to share advice and information related to language arts instruction (Hopkins & Lowenhaupt, 2013). They rarely, if ever, shared advice and information about mathematics instruction or instruction related to other subject areas. This trend was due, at least in part, to school leaders' and teachers' beliefs that mathematics, in particular, was less linguistically challenging for students learning English. This is a common misconception (Bahr & de Garcia, 2010) that has implications for the design and implementation of educational infrastructures for ELLs.

Figure 4.2 shows the subject-specific instructional advice and information networks among school staff in one of Twin Rivers' fourteen elementary schools. Whereas ESL teachers were just as likely to provide and seek instructional advice related to language arts as other staff members, they were significantly less likely to provide or seek instructional advice related to other school subjects, especially mathematics. Moreover, ESL teachers served as brokers of language arts instructional advice and information among general education teachers, meaning that their absence in the network would have resulted in less language arts advice-sharing among other teachers. By virtue of their interactions with ESL teachers, then, general education teachers were better positioned to learn how to support ELLs in English language arts than any other subject, where their opportunities to learn from ESL teachers were limited. Whereas district and school norms supported seeking out ESL teachers for advice about language arts instruction, they did not support similar instructional advice- and information-seeking from ESL teachers for other school subjects. These differences are consequential for teachers' capacity to support ELLs in meeting the learning goals outlined in the CCSS and NGSS, especially in math and science. And they are troubling when considering particular populations of students who tend to be underrepresented in STEM (science, technology, engineering, and mathematics) fields.

## CONCLUSION

Local implementation of standards and accountability has been a perennial problem for education policy. The challenge is in great part a function of the weakness and unevenness in the local educational infrastructures that structure district policymakers', school leaders', and teachers' efforts to make sense of standards; figure out their entailments for classroom instruction; and

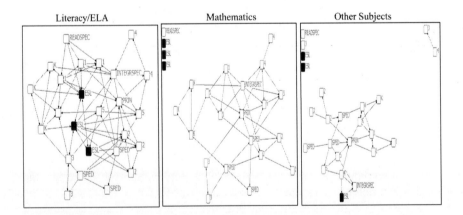

**Figure 4.2.  Pine Elementary School social network diagrams by subject, 2011, revealing frequent interactions between ESL and general education teachers related to language arts instruction, yet virtually no interaction related to instruction in mathematics or other subjects.**

redesign instructional practice and improvement efforts accordingly. This chapter focused on how educational infrastructure differs dramatically even within the same school or school district, depending on the school subject. As such, policymakers and practitioners alike should think carefully about how educational infrastructures for supporting classroom instruction, maintaining instructional quality, and creating opportunities for peer learning among teachers differ by school subject.

For local policymakers and educators grappling with what CCSS and NGSS might mean for their schools and classrooms, the educational infrastructure should be a major consideration. Locals must examine how their educational infrastructures support (1) teachers and school leaders learning about what CCSS and NGSS mean for their practice and (2) teachers' and school leaders' efforts to put the ideas learned into practice. Further, locals must systematically examine how their educational infrastructures differ by school subject and consider the consequences of these differences for school leaders' and teachers' opportunities to learn from and about instruction as they work with CCSS and NGSS, depending on the school subject. A systematic analysis of subject matter differences in educational infrastructures for supporting instruction, professional learning about instruction, and instructional improvement will help identify potential implementation challenges for CCSS and NGSS. Such analysis could be the basis for redesigning aspects of the educational infrastructure for particular school subjects so as to better support school leaders and teachers learning from and about instruction. Working with finite resources means, of course, that infrastructure redesign will involve some difficult trade-offs.

*Part 2 Introduction*

# Leading Standards Enactment in Classrooms

## Jonathan A. Supovitz

The ways in which teachers take up the challenge of standards implementation will have a major effect on the ultimate legacy of the Common Core State Standards (CCSS) movement. How can state, district, and school leaders support standards implementation in classrooms? What leadership strategies, resources, and tools do they have at their disposal to help teachers to understand some of the important distinctions between the CCSS and prior incarnations of standards and to foster deep implementation of standards-aligned instruction? In this section we focus on some of the material, human, and social resources that leaders have to support the enactment of standards in classrooms. As the authors of the chapters in this section point out, the field has learned quite a bit about the role of curriculum, professional development, and assessment practices that show how these support materials interact with instruction to produce powerful teaching and student learning.

The section begins with two very different chapters that examine the processes and implications of curriculum decisions made by districts and schools that help to shape the experiences of students. In chapter 5, Janine Remillard and Joshua Taton of the University of Pennsylvania identify, examine, and dispel three common myths about the role of curriculum in standards implementation. They argue that leaders and teachers can both over-rely and under-rely on curriculum materials in change efforts and offer both different frames to think about curricular decisions and specific advice for leaders grappling with curricular choices. In doing so, they situate curriculum in an appropriate place in the standards implementation puzzle.

. The CCSS movement also means that the marketplace will soon be inundated with a slew of revised curriculum materials that claim Common Core alignment. But it's buyer beware, warns Morgan Polikoff of the University of Southern California in chapter 6. Polikoff provides an overview of different ways that district and school leaders can think about testing claims of alignment between curriculum and standards. He outlines a systemic approach to analyzing curricular/standards alignment that schools or districts might use in the textbook- or materials-adoption process.

One of the key intentions of the standards developers is the promise of more rigorous experiences for all students. This combines the potential of both higher quality activities and more equitable experiences for students. In chapter 7, Emily Hodge of Montclair State University in New Jersey delves into the intriguing case of one district's early experiences with implementing the Common Core. She identifies some of the unanticipated conflicts that arise with efforts to fulfill the promise of rigor for all students. In doing so, Hodge identifies some of the important underlying assumptions within traditional modes of school organization that implementers of the CCSS must confront in order to fulfill the promise of high expectations for all students.

America is a melting pot of diverse schools and inevitably the culture of these organizations will influence how they engage with the CCSS. In chapter 8, Bruce Fuller, of U.C. Berkeley and director of Policy Analysis for California Education (PACE), discusses the growing presence of what he calls "uncommon schools" that are increasingly dotting the American landscape—including small high schools, charter schools, and magnet schools with a variety of specialized themes. Fuller observes that the particular mission and professional coherence of the faculties inside of these different types of schools will influence the ways in which the standards take root. Through his discussion, he surfaces a series of interesting tools and resources of which uncommon school leaders and faculty can take advantage in order to best capitalize on the CCSS movement.

Teaching to the CCSS, of course, requires teachers to be learners as well as teachers. In chapter 9, Vivian Mihalakis and Anthony Petrosky of the Institute for Learning (IFL) at the University of Pittsburgh describe the IFL's approach to building teachers' understanding of the cognitively demanding tasks advocated by the CCSS. To convey their professional development ideas, they share the organization's experiences with providing professional development for teachers in English language arts workshops across the country through putting teachers in the role of learners to understand how instructors can convey the expectations with the CCSS. Using the example of Martin Luther King's "I have a dream" speech, they make important distinctions of what are cognitively demanding tasks for students and what this implies for instructional decision making.

Here are several questions for you and your colleagues to discuss to better lead standards enactment in classrooms:

1. How does your district or school use curriculum in its improvement efforts? What latitude do teachers have to choose curriculum and supplemental materials?
2. How do you assess the degree to which your curriculum and materials are aligned to standards?
3. How are professional development experiences in your system organized to put adults in the position of learners in order to understand the implications of the CCSS?
4. What policies and practices (i.e., instructional grouping, how teachers talk about and use test data) might send inconsistent signals about the importance of high expectations for all students?
5. How might you use the CCSS as a tool to inspire deeper learning by teachers and students alike?

*Chapter Five*

# Rewriting Myths about Curriculum Materials and Teaching to New Standards

Janine Remillard and Joshua Taton

Myths are stories people use to help make sense of the world around them. Although myths can provide insight into cultural beliefs and values, they also perpetuate misconceptions. As with all myths, those that emerge in education weave together factual realities, partial truths, and full-blown falsehoods. In order to take informed actions, school leaders must scrutinize these myths and sort out truth from lore. The challenge is to honor the wisdom found in myths, while bringing their fallacies to light. In doing so, leaders can rewrite the myths that sometimes guide decisions in schools.

This chapter is concerned with educational myths about curriculum programs and teachers. Because curriculum programs are an established component of the fabric of education, school leaders routinely oversee curriculum decisions. For many, this task translates into managing the adoption of curriculum programs and resources—textbooks, teacher guides, software packages, supplementary practice books, and more. Making sound curriculum decisions—that is, selecting curriculum packages that are skillfully designed and aligned with the aims of the district, and then implementing them in effective ways—has never been straightforward or without controversy. In today's climate of demanding standards, accountability measures, as well as an ever-expanding universe of resources marketed to districts and teachers, the task seems formidable, even Herculean.

This chapter explores three common myths about curriculum resources and teaching that circulate in schools and often influence the curriculum decisions made by leaders and teachers. Like most myths, these three have been with us for generations, but each is now being recast in the language of new standards or via the explosion of available resources. Because these myths contain some wisdom and partial truths, mingled with pure fiction, they may lead practitioners down precarious paths. The aim here is to expose troubling elements of these myths and offer alternative narratives to guide practice.

The discussion of each myth concludes with two types of recommendations for school leaders. The first offers a way to reframe the myth or recast it under different terms. Following these recommendations involves adapting one's framework or generating a new one for informing future actions. The second type of recommendation is more technical in nature and offers specific actions leaders might take in rewriting the myth.[1] In reality, the two must occur hand in hand, like the two faces of the Roman god Janus, honoring the concrete in the abstract and the general in the particular.

Before moving on to the myths, a brief note about definitions: In this chapter, the term *curriculum program* (and sometimes *curriculum*) refers to intentionally designed resources for teachers that set out an instructional pathway through a specific subject, such as Algebra I or fifth-grade English Language Arts. Other terms, often used similarly, include *teacher's guide*, *textbook*, or *curriculum materials*. Instructional *resource* refers to individual instructional activities or tools that might or might not be part of a larger curriculum program. *Curriculum resource* is a more general term, used to refer to the broad category of curriculum tools designed to support instruction.

## MYTH #1: GOOD TEACHERS DON'T USE PREPARED CURRICULUM PROGRAMS; INSTEAD, THEY DESIGN THEIR OWN

*"In our district, teachers, not textbooks, teach children."*

*"Now that we have the new standards that specify what students should learn at each grade level, these have become our curriculum. Teachers follow them to design their lessons."*

The myth that good teachers have the Midas touch and therefore don't need curriculum programs has been around for decades. This myth paints teachers as curricular experts who are best positioned to create instructional plans tailored to particular students. It also reflects the prevalence of low-quality and uninspired textbook series that have dominated the market throughout the latter half of the twentieth century. Some packages simply did not have much to offer, while others talked down to teachers, as the oft-used phrase "teacher-proof curriculum" suggests.

The perception that good teachers reject textbooks and design their own curriculum has been a persistent belief of educators over the years. Researchers have long noted unease about using teacher's guides among many teachers, regardless of whether the curriculum in question was a traditional textbook from the 1980s (Ball & Feiman-Nemser, 1988) or a more innovative program reflecting the vision outlined in the widely adopted National Council of Teachers of Mathematics Standards of the 1990s (Lloyd, 1999; Remillard & Bryans, 2004).

Under the current era of the Common Core State Standards, this myth is playing out in some districts and schools in a different way. Teachers are encouraged to use the new standards as their guide for *what* to teach and are expected to gather and develop instructional resources to determine *how*. Curriculum resources of any kind are viewed as unnecessary, redundant to what teachers *already* do or *should* be doing.

This myth has great appeal. It is embraced and retold because it treats teachers' expertise with great reverence. This is its wisdom: Teachers are critical curriculum designers and are well positioned to tailor instructional designs to the needs of their particular students. When measured against curriculum materials, teachers win every time. Curriculum programs might be taken up as an impermanent solution during periods of transition, or for inexperienced teachers, but moving away from relying on them is generally viewed as the ultimate goal.

When taken to its logical conclusion, though, the fallacy of this myth quickly emerges: Curriculum materials and teachers do not do the same type of work. In short, this myth is based on and promotes an image of teachers as solo performers and of curriculum programs as props or scripts. Although these perceptions appear to honor teachers, they actually work against teaching and school improvement.

Revising this myth requires a careful look at the distinct contributions that *well-designed*[2] curriculum programs and skilled teachers offer to the enactment of instruction. Doing so can lead to a reframing of the teacher-curriculum relationship as a collaborative or participatory one (Remillard, 2005). Through making sense of and planning with curriculum guides, teachers immerse themselves in a partnership with the authors—a partnership to which both members contribute in mutual and complementary ways.

In their work, curriculum authors draw on a "big picture" map of the curriculum and an understanding of how concepts and skills develop over time and in relation to one another. This map is informed by knowledge of content and research on learning. The curriculum development process typically involves rounds of field testing in real classrooms; developers are able to incorporate insights from these trials in their revisions, including knowledge of how students are likely to respond to given tasks.

Teachers, on the other hand, bring to this partnership indispensable knowledge of their particular context and students, their prior knowledge and experiences, and their own learning needs. By drawing on their own experience, expertise, and pedagogical skills, along with local resources when planning with curriculum materials, teachers make adaptations to suit their students' needs and, when enacting the curriculum, they steer interactions with students through important content.

## Rewriting the Myth: Good Teachers Partner with Curriculum Resources

Recasting this myth involves actively reframing good teaching as partnering with curriculum authors. School leaders can initiate this reframing by encouraging teachers to use curriculum guides as tools and resources in planning instruction and as anchors when enacting lessons. Teachers' expertise must be seen as essential to curriculum use rather than in conflict with it. Moreover, deliberative, purposeful use of curriculum materials can be recognized as a form of expertise to be fostered.

## Strategies for School Leaders

1. Create opportunities for teachers to explore, deliberate about, and work with curriculum resources in collaboration with colleagues. Specific lessons, representations, or instructional approaches in curriculum guides can provide a basis for productive inquiry in a professional learning community.
2. Consider selecting curriculum materials that are thoughtfully designed and respectful of teachers' expertise. Curriculum programs vary in the extent to which they engage with teachers as professionals. Materials that are transparent about design rationales and intended learning pathways support reasoned deliberation and customization more than guides that simply prescribe teacher actions.

## MYTH #2: THE SINGLE-CURRICULUM APPROACH IS OBSOLETE: CURATING RESOURCES FROM THE DIGITAL MARKETPLACE IS THE WAY TO GO

*"A perfect textbook doesn't exist, and there are so many good lessons and activities online. We encourage teachers to take advantage of these resources and pull lessons from different sources."*

*"Some of the best lessons I have found were posted by real teachers on their websites or even Pinterest."*

The myth that a stronger and more flexible curriculum can be built by mixing and matching resources gathered from a range of sources may emanate from a long-standing proclivity for eclecticism. It has gained prominence with the growth of the Internet. Prior to the emergence of the web as a medium for social, professional, and commercial exchange, curriculum materials typically entered schools and classrooms through a single gateway, as the officially adopted textbook (Remillard & Heck, 2014). Teachers' use of additional material was usually supplemental to the core text.

Today's digital environment and web-based economy has greatly expanded the availability of new resources and given teachers direct access to tools and ideas beyond the district-adopted program. For many teachers and some leaders, this phenomenon presents an exciting opportunity: the freedom and flexibility to compile a customized curriculum that takes advantage of a wide variety of resources (many of which are free). It can also be seductive because of the low cost. But due to the uncertain quality of such resources and the potential programmatic incoherence they introduce, this approach runs the risk of opening Pandora's box.

As with most myths, this narrative is not entirely false. It acknowledges that a single curriculum program cannot meet all the needs of a district, and it recognizes the vast and growing array of alternatives available to teachers. Like the first myth, it values teachers' professional judgment to select appropriate resources for their students. Unlike the first myth, teachers and instructional resources are not seen as redundant; rather, the assumption is that teachers can benefit from using resources selectively.

This myth places great value on flexibility, variety, and individual choice. Some have characterized the teacher's role in this new digital marketplace as one of curator: Not only does the teacher accumulate and maintain the collection of resources but she designs the students' encounters with them.

The danger of this myth is that it is based on a one-dimensional view of curriculum—as a collection of discrete options in a smorgasbord of activities. Even if each activity is of high quality and has worthy instructional goals, this framing ignores the second critical dimension of curriculum—a coherent map of the goals and how they relate to and build on one another. In short, the myth of the mix-and-match curriculum undermines the need for attention to the long view of curriculum organization, including how concepts and ideas are sequenced to build over time.

A fundamental aspect of the new standards is the articulation of learning progressions across grade levels. These pathways map the development of key concepts and skills as they increase in complexity and sophistication over time. This perspective on curriculum emphasizes cohesion across topics, concepts, and ideas. Foundations laid down in earlier grades can be built upon in following years.

When guided by the curriculum-smorgasbord myth, two types of incoherence are likely to result. One is an arrangement in which teachers individually curate their own curriculum by hunting and gathering resources from multiple sources allows for considerable variation in experience among classes at any grade level. The other, greater risk, however, is fracturing the planned progression of concepts across grades. This risk can be reduced when teachers or even districts work collectively to build a coherent curriculum map.[3]

An alternative framing for how teachers might navigate the vast marketplace of resources emphasizes this *mapping* over curating. A map, after all, represents a particular region, depicting both the elements within the region *and* the relationships among them. It offers possible journeys from place to place. Curriculum mapping requires attention to the pathways between concepts and not simply the concepts to be learned. Using a curriculum map to scrutinize instructional resources should involve assessing the quality and fit of each instructional task and judging the placement of all tasks in relation to one another.

## Rewriting the Myth: From Curriculum Curating to Curriculum Mapping

Recasting this myth provides an opportunity for leaders to bring attention to the value of guiding curriculum maps and the need for coherence across grades. Finding and leveraging high-quality resources from the Internet and assembling them into a coherent and purposeful curriculum is certainly possible. It must be done at the school or district level, however, or by empowered committees of teachers both within and across grade levels, rather than by teachers acting independently.

### Strategies for School Leaders

1. Make an explicit curriculum map for each content area that represents the progressions for growth over time. Use documents associated with the Common Core State Standards and the Next Generation Science Standards, or other resources, to identify how curriculum structures progress across grades. Consultation with outside experts can also help minimize programmatic incoherence.
2. Promote judicious and deliberative use of found resources. Encourage teachers to collaboratively discuss supplementation and modifications, using the curriculum map as a guide.
3. Provide opportunities for curricular conversations among teachers across grade levels. Teachers who teach the same grade are often given common planning time, allowing them to coordinate instruction for the short term. It is less common to encourage cross-level curriculum planning, which emphasizes attending to the long view of student learning.

MYTH #3: WHEN IT COMES TO MEETING NEW STANDARDS,
THE MOST CRITICAL INVESTMENT SCHOOL LEADERS CAN
MAKE IS TO ADOPT A WELL-ALIGNED CURRICULUM
PROGRAM (AKA IMPROVEMENT THROUGH ADOPTION)

*"After extensive review of all the options out there, we selected a curriculum that we believe will do the best job of meeting our learning goals and is straightforward for teachers to use."*

*"Along with our Common Core-aligned math program, we purchased a Learning Management System to monitor student growth and help our teachers stay on track."*

Unlike the previous myths, this narrative embraces a single-program approach and acknowledges that curriculum programs play a valuable role in facilitating instructional improvement. After all, curriculum materials can easily be placed in the hands of every teacher in a system; moreover, they provide guidance on the day-to-day decisions of what should be taught, in what sequence, and, in many cases, how. For these reasons, curriculum programs are critical to maintaining coherence across schools and classrooms. From this standpoint, curriculum programs are viewed as key levers of instructional change and important for meeting goals set by new standards.

The curriculum-adoption myth has guided district policy and budgeting for many years. The widespread adoption of the Common Core Standards has sparked an explosion of new curriculum programs, supplementary materials, and other tools, produced by the multibillion-dollar textbook industry, which is downright indiscriminate in its use of the "CCSS-aligned" signet.

School districts invest substantial time and human resources, examining available programs and then selecting those that appear to fit best with their expectations and needs. And then they spend millions of dollars on materials for each classroom.

In recent years, the curriculum adoption myth has expanded to include a variety of learning management systems (LMS), which schools can adopt in conjunction with curriculum programs. These online management systems are designed to support use of a curriculum package and, at substantial additional cost, offer pacing guides and assessments and track progress toward learning goals. Unsurprisingly, the rollout of the Common Core Standards prompted an emergence of new management systems available for purchase.

Like the other myths, this one rests on a partial truth. Curriculum programs that are well designed and aligned to the standards offer a valuable base and guide for teachers, and they can contribute to much-needed coherence, as described in the previous section. The fallacy of this myth, as it commonly plays out in school systems, is that curriculum adoption itself is treated as the pivotal investment. In other words, once adopted, curriculum programs do the bulk of the necessary work. But viewing curriculum programs and related tools as the sole solution often becomes the Achilles' heel of district leaders.

The problem is the assumption that implementing new curriculum materials is a straightforward matter of simply getting them into the hands of teachers and students. This assumption misses two key variables that can make or break the investment. The first is the people, primarily teachers, whose on-the-ground decisions and actions are critical to successful implementation. In order to use a curriculum package productively, teachers need ongoing opportunities to examine it fully, learn about new approaches, and reflect on students' encounters with it.

The second variable is how well the package fits within the existing paradigm of the school system. For a curriculum package to be implemented successfully, it should mesh with the prevailing pedagogical perspective and stance on mathematics in the district. Curriculum packages are not like a Procrustean bed—one size does *not* fit all.

Recasting the adoption myth involves framing curriculum implementation as an adaptive process. This idea extends the view, discussed previously, of curriculum use as a partnership. It also draws on the concept of mutual adaptation described by Berman and McLaughlin (1978). They found that new innovations worked best when implementation involved making adaptations to the new program to suit local circumstances, along with adjustments and learning in the local setting. From this perspective, incorporating a new curriculum into a system requires active engagement, new learning, and adjustments on the part of teachers and other professionals. This view is akin to the notion that implementing new initiatives should be treated as a constructive process, requiring meaning-making and judgment on the part of those enacting the change (Supovitz & Spillane, this volume).

Taking an adaptive view of curriculum implementation goes beyond engaging the actors in the system; it also implicates the system itself. New curriculum programs and instructional resources interact with those already in place. Their use is also affected by existing programmatic practices and structures, such as classroom routines and norms, assessment practices, and class schedules. In short, purchasing a new curriculum program or LMS has a financial cost, but incorporating that program into a school system requires an investment of time and resources as well as a willingness to support professional engagement and self-examination. The payoff will reflect the quality of the investment.

## Rewriting the Myth: From Curriculum Adoption to Program Adaptation

Reframing curriculum adoption as *program adaptation* involves seeing the selection decision as one component in a complex process of school improvement. School improvement, writ large, involves additional investments in developing and articulating a common vision, building staff capacity, and modifying local practices and structures, as outlined above. Adopting a new curriculum program can catalyze these activities, but it cannot replace them. School leaders can use curriculum adoption cycles as opportunities to engage an entire community in examining the curriculum and engaging in self-assessment.

## Strategies for School Leaders

1. Make curriculum adaptation activities a centerpiece of professional activity and professional development. When a new program is being considered or adopted, establish time and support for teachers to collectively explore it, understand its implications for their existing practices, and thoughtfully plan adaptations. These opportunities need to persist over time, not terminate at the adoption date, allowing for ongoing reflection and refinement even well after a program has been selected.
2. Consider the costs of adaptive activities described above and anticipate them when building a budget for curriculum adoption.

## CONCLUSION: CHANGING THE CONVERSATION

This chapter has identified three persistent myths about curriculum resources and their role in teaching and schools. Although these are not the only prevailing myths about curriculum resources, they are common and powerful ones that influence practice and policy in explicit and subtle ways. Like all myths, they weave together partial truths and messages of wisdom but also contain troubling assumptions.

The goal of this chapter has been to examine these myths, sort out fact from fiction, and offer alternative narratives to guide practice. Across these rewritten myths, several themes emerge that can help change the conversation about what curriculum resources are, what they offer to schools, and the opportunities they provide school leaders.

First, *curriculum resources are tools* in the hands of professionals. They cannot replace teachers or quality teaching; moreover, they cannot create professional expertise in schools. Instead, when curriculum resources are well designed and appropriately selected and used, they serve as valuable tools that can enhance professional expertise. But, like all tools, they are not self-enacting.

The second theme is more subtle than the first; it is about the *type* of tool curriculum resources are. It helps to think of them as partners in instructional design. As tools intentionally developed to support instruction, they can bring new insight, approaches, frameworks, and knowledge into classrooms and schools. Using these tools allows teachers to engage with new models and representations, different ways to organize content, and novel pedagogical strategies. Well-designed curriculum resources are informed by research findings on student learning and have been field tested by many teachers. *As design partners, curriculum resources provide teachers access to knowledge and processes beyond their immediate experience.*

The third theme builds on the second: using new tools typically requires change. The change needed might involve new learning opportunities for staff or the development of new structures or routines. It might involve rethinking existing practices. In other words, *although new curriculum resources have the potential to infuse novel ideas into a school, their success depends on the capacity of those using the tools.*

Because curriculum programs are an established component of schooling, school leaders can use their selection and adoption opportunistically to catalyze cycles of collective reflection and growth.

## NOTES

1. The two types of recommendations reflect the distinction between technical and adaptive challenges made by Heifetz, Linsky & Grashow (2009) and Supovitz (this volume). Following Supovitz, an argument of this chapter is that school leaders' actions must be both technical and adaptive.

2. Not all curriculum programs are designed with equal care or expertise. Well-designed materials are based on research findings and undergo rounds of field testing and revision. They assume teachers will make adaptive decisions and provide support for teachers to do so. For guidance on curriculum materials aligned with the Common Core Standards, leaders are encouraged to consult documents on the CCSS website that contains criteria for developing CCSS-based programs.

3. For an example, see Gewertz (2014).

## Chapter Six

# Overcoming the Challenges of Choosing Curriculum Materials

*A Systematic Approach to Evaluating Common Core Alignment*

## Morgan S. Polikoff

Even though publishers were quick to slap "Common Core Aligned!" stickers on their curriculum materials after the standards were adopted, such claims are often misleading (Herold & Molna, 2014). This lack of credible information on alignment represents one of the biggest challenges of implementing the standards. Complicating matters, the sheer number of curriculum materials—textbooks, units, and lessons—is on the rise. Because no one independently rates the alignment of this growing body of materials—whether commercial or noncommercial, traditional or online—schools are left to fend for themselves.

Recognizing the problem, EdReports and a handful of other organizations have begun evaluating the alignment of curriculum materials to standards. While promising, such initiatives will not achieve their full goals for some time. And even then, they will analyze only a subset of the available materials, and likely not many of the free online lessons. Meanwhile, schools and districts have to make decisions with the information they have, even as teachers and administrators say they lack the information they need to make smart choices.

It doesn't have to be this way. Systematic approaches exist for making these kinds of decisions. This chapter offers specific guidance for making decisions in choosing curriculum materials and addressing their shortcomings before and during implementation. And it does so in a way that enables school leaders to use the decision-making process to build rich understanding of the standards while also involving teachers deeply in key policy and practice decisions.

To be sure, educators have always had methods for evaluating alignment. However, these methods have generally not been described or supported in research, so the feasibility and validity of these rating systems are unclear. Furthermore, there is no evidence that these methods have been, or can be, applied systematically at scale, limiting their utility for influencing decisions outside of isolated cases.

Developing and systematically applying a common approach to analyzing materials could result in widespread adoption of quality materials that can help teachers meet the standards and improve instruction and student outcomes.

## MEASURING THE ALIGNMENT OF CURRICULUM MATERIALS WITH STANDARDS

The recommended approach to analyzing alignment is described in the next section. First, though, is a brief overview of various approaches used to analyze the content of curriculum materials to assess their alignment with standards such as the Common Core.

### Approaches That Haven't Been Peer Reviewed

Ideally, the process for aligning materials with standards would start with the writing of the materials. Textbook publishers often use their own methods for aligning their materials to the standards, but publishers don't describe their methods, so the quality is unclear. Some textbook publishers report research on the alignment of their books to the standards on their websites. For example, McGraw-Hill Education's website for Everyday Math advertises 100 percent alignment with the CCSS. While publishers' alignment reports may be accurate based on their own methodologies, recent investigations by independent researchers suggest claims of alignment are likely overstated (Herold & Molna, 2014).

Online resources also exist for individuals looking to evaluate the alignment of materials to the standards. Student Achievement Partners, founded by some of the CCSS writers, offers the Instructional Materials Evaluation Toolkit. The toolkit uses a multistep process to help evaluators identify nonnegotiable items from the CCSS, rating skill alignment with the CCSS, and ranking several "quality" items on their degree of alignment. Though comprehensive, there is no information available about the technical quality of these ratings, nor is it clear whether these approaches are feasible for educators to use at wide scale.

## Peer-Reviewed Approaches

One content analysis strategy used in peer-reviewed research is to count the number of pages or problems devoted to a specific topic and compare it with a target. For example, one might note that the fourth-grade Common Core math standards have one objective out of thirty-seven that addresses multiplication of whole numbers (approximately 3 percent) and count the number of pages in a set of textbooks on that topic, comparing that proportion to 3 percent. The counting strategy has been used to evaluate the alignment of U.S. textbooks with achievement tests.

While straightforward and feasible, the page-counting approach is limited in at least three ways. First, it assumes that each objective is of equal weight. Second, the topic descriptions used are generally very coarse. And third, it ignores the cognitive demand aspect of content: For instance, are students expected to perform multiplication procedures or demonstrate understanding of whole-number multiplication? To address cognitive demand, sometimes the page-counting approach is supplemented by analyzing related measures, such as the amount of problems versus narrative text and the manner in which text is presented (pictorial/graphic versus textual).

Task analysis, which focuses on the nature of the tasks offered in a set of curriculum materials, is another commonly used evaluation strategy. Task analysis methods recognize that in addition to presentation in text, tasks depend on teacher implementation and student practice. Content analysis is therefore only a small portion of the task analysis model.

Textbooks may be analyzed in a task analysis model for features like the physical characteristics of the book, the structure of the lessons, and the nature of the problems. Problems may then be evaluated on contextual features (purely mathematical content, real-world application, etc.), manipulative features, and methods of computation (mental math, standard algorithm, etc.). While task analyses can provide useful evidence, they are not explicitly useful for examining alignment because they are not tied to any analysis of standards and do not come with an alignment methodology. Further, given the number of dimensions to be rated, this approach may be too complex for educators to use across a range of materials.

A third type of content analysis strategy is a hybrid of the counting and task analysis approaches. This involves coding text in terms of its content coverage and comparing that analysis to a coding of the standards to which the text is intended to be aligned. The Surveys of Enacted Curriculum, which is described in more detail below, is an example of one such strategy. Hybrid approaches typically measure both content and cognitive demand, and they have a good deal of evidence behind them. While this evidence suggests teachers can understand and use the methods, these approaches have primarily been used by researchers rather than practitioners.

The remainder of this chapter outlines a framework for using these hybrid content analysis approaches to analyze the alignment of curriculum materials with the Common Core standards. Not only can this approach be used to analyze materials, but it can also be a powerful tool for building teachers' understanding of the standards, the materials they have chosen, and the gaps that invariably arise in any set of materials, in the hopes of addressing those gaps through supplementary materials.

## A SYSTEMATIC APPROACH TO ANALYZING CURRICULUM MATERIALS

The approach described here is based on the Surveys of Enacted Curriculum, a set of tools that have been used by researchers, state and district policymakers, and teachers for over a decade.[1] The primary use of the Surveys of Enacted Curriculum has been to rate the alignment among teachers' instruction, content standards, and assessments of student achievement. Research indicates that teachers understand and can make use of the content languages, that the alignment results based on the Surveys of Enacted Curriculum predict student achievement gains, and that teachers can use alignment data to improve their instruction.

The heart of the Surveys of Enacted Curriculum is a set of content languages, one in each subject area, designed to cover all the content a teacher might teach in K–12 mathematics, science, and English language arts. The languages define content at the intersection of specific topics and levels of cognitive demand. For instance, in mathematics, topics include multiply decimals, area and volume, and quadratic equations. The five cognitive demand levels in mathematics are:

- Memorize/recall;
- Perform procedures;
- Demonstrate/communicate understanding;
- Conjecture/analyze/generalize; and
- Integrate/synthesize/critique.

The languages are defined on the Surveys of Enacted Curriculum website, www.seconline.org, and a number of background resources and training materials are also available there.

### Analyzing Materials

The Surveys of Enacted Curriculum content languages are used to analyze curriculum materials, standards, and assessments. The general approach for analyzing a document proceeds in eight steps.

1. **Identify two or more people to conduct the analysis.** The content analysis procedure can be a useful professional development activity for deeply studying a document, as it provides a clear, neutral, and systematic way to understand the topics and cognitive demands called for in the standards or curriculum material. More than one person is desirable because individuals often have different interpretations of content, because it is more reliable if multiple people are used, and because it may enhance the professional learning opportunity.

2. **Decide whether content analysis will be done together (a consensus approach) or independently.** The typical approach begins with coding the materials independently. Next, areas of disagreement are discussed before final coding decisions are made. Ultimately, the results are averaged across reviewers. However, a consensus approach, where participants must negotiate and reach agreement, should produce similar results and may be a better collaborative learning experience.

3. **Select the target document to be analyzed** (for example, the Common Core standards for fourth-grade mathematics).

4. **Break the document into "chunks" to be analyzed.** Most documents will have natural chunks. For instance, in a set of standards, the most typical chunk is the objective. In a textbook, chunks will include text boxes at the start of a lesson and problems at the end of a lesson. Each chunk will be equally weighted by default (in other words, each chunk is worth one point), but it's possible to choose any weighting scheme.

5. **Analyze the document one chunk at a time.** For each chunk, decide what combinations of topic and cognitive demand are covered. Typically, no more than six combinations of topic and cognitive demand are allowed for any one chunk.

6. **Divide the one point per chunk equally among the topics and cognitive demand levels covered.** For instance, if a textbook problem covers multiply decimals at the level of memorize/recall and at the level of perform procedures, each of those two topic/cognitive demand combinations would receive half a point.

7. **Do this approach for the whole document.** At the end, calculate the percent of total points on each topic and cognitive demand level—this can easily be done with Excel or other spreadsheet software. Those percentages have interpretations like "2.5% of the document is on multiply decimals at the level of perform procedures."

8. **Repeat steps three through seven for the comparison document** (for example, a particular fourth-grade mathematics textbook).

The result of the eight steps will be two content analyses, one for the instructional target and one for the materials. Each analysis will break down the content in the document in terms of its topic and cognitive demand coverage.

## Calculating Alignment

To determine alignment, compare the document analyses in steps seven and eight. There are two typical ways of estimating alignment. One asks, "What percent of each document is in exact proportional agreement with the other document?" The other asks, "What percent of the content in document A (for example, the textbook) is content that's also in document B (for example, the standards)?" The first alignment index is the one that has typically been used in research, but the second relaxes the potentially problematic assumption that each standard should be weighted equally. Both indices are proportions ranging from 0 (complete misalignment) to 1 (complete alignment).

To illustrate these alignment calculations, consider figure 6.1, which shows simplified analyses for a textbook and set of standards. The figure breaks down the content in a textbook and a set of standards across four topics. So, for example, the top left cell indicates that 5 percent of the textbook content is on multiply fractions at the level of memorize.

To calculate the first alignment index, simply compare the two documents one cell at a time, take the minimum of each comparison, and sum them. Again, this can easily be done in Excel. Reading across the top row, for instance, these minimums would be .05, .05, .05, 0, 0. Doing this for all cells results in a value of .75, indicating 75 percent alignment.

To calculate the second alignment index, find all the cells for the textbook that are covered at all in the standards, and add across them. Doing this gives a value of .95 (the only textbook content that isn't in the standards is the 5 percent on multiply decimals at the level of demonstrate). So 95 percent of the textbook content is also in the standards. One could also flip this calculation, finding all the cells in the standards that are covered at all in the textbook. This would also give a value of .95 (the only standards content that isn't in the textbooks is the 5 percent on multiply fractions at the conjecture level). Thus, we would conclude that 95 percent of standards content is covered by the textbook.

The content analysis data also allow you to describe the content of the textbook and standards in other important ways. For instance, 25 percent of the textbook content in this example is on multiply fractions, while 35 percent is on divide fractions. And 80 percent of the textbook content is on memorization and procedures. These descriptive indicators can stimulate interesting and important conversations among district policymakers, administrators, and teachers; for instance, should 25 percent of instructional time be spent on multiplying fractions, just because that is what the book says?

| Textbook | Memorize | Procedures | Demonstrate | Conjecture | Integrate |
|---|---|---|---|---|---|
| Multiply fractions | 0.05 | 0.15 | 0.05 | 0.00 | 0.00 |
| Divide fractions | 0.10 | 0.20 | 0.05 | 0.00 | 0.00 |
| Multiply decimals | 0.05 | 0.10 | 0.05 | 0.00 | 0.00 |
| Divide decimals | 0.10 | 0.05 | 0.05 | 0.00 | 0.00 |

| Standards | Memorize | Procedures | Demonstrate | Conjecture | Integrate |
|---|---|---|---|---|---|
| Multiply fractions | 0.05 | 0.05 | 0.05 | 0.05 | 0.00 |
| Divide fractions | 0.10 | 0.10 | 0.10 | 0.00 | 0.00 |
| Multiply decimals | 0.10 | 0.15 | 0.00 | 0.00 | 0.00 |
| Divide decimals | 0.10 | 0.10 | 0.05 | 0.00 | 0.00 |

**Figure 6.1.  Sample content analysis data for calculating alignment.**

What other mathematical content is shortchanged by weighting fractions so heavily? Does the heavy focus on memorization and procedures match the standards?

## An Example of Textbook Analysis

Following the procedure described above, a previous study (Polikoff, 2014) examined the alignment of fourth-grade mathematics textbooks claiming to be "Common Core-aligned" to the fourth-grade mathematics standards. Four textbooks were chosen: *GO Math!*, *enVisionMATH*, *Math Connects*, and *Saxon Math*. Three analysts examined the materials and the standards and rated them using the procedure described above. The results were analyzed by calculating the alignment indices, also described above, and by exploring the documents in terms of their coverage of topics and cognitive demand levels of interest.

The results, shown in table 6.1, provide useful information about differences in alignment. For instance, it is clear that *GO Math!* and *enVision-MATH* had considerably higher alignment on both indices than *Math Connects* and *Saxon Math*. Also, the second alignment index, as expected, produced much higher values than the first index. For instance, the top right value in the table indicates that 79.8 percent of the content in *GO Math!* was also in the Common Core math standards. This is about 15 percentage points more than *Saxon*.

The data were also analyzed descriptively to explore areas of alignment and misalignment. Doing so indicates that cognitive demand is a major

**Table 6.1.  Alignment results from comparison of textbook with Common Core fourth-grade mathematics standards.**

| Textbook | Alignment Index 1 | Alignment Index 2 |
|---|---|---|
| GO Math! Common Core | 0.396 | 0.798 |
| Math Connects Common Core | 0.291 | 0.675 |
| enVisionMATH Common Core | 0.357 | 0.765 |
| Saxon Intermediate | 0.282 | 0.647 |

source of misalignment for all textbooks. While only 60 percent of the content in the Common Core math standards at fourth grade is on memorization or procedures, 87 percent to 93 percent of the content in each of the four textbooks is on those skills. Districts choosing any of these books would have to supplement in order to give students access to higher-order cognitive demands.

## Extending beyond Textbooks: Suggestions for Implementation

The procedures described here may seem daunting on a first read, but there are several ways to make the process more manageable. One approach is for districts to work together on these analyses. A great advantage of nearly national standards is that the results will hold across states. Collaborative relationships among districts can reduce the analysis burden and may lead to common adoption decisions, which could improve implementation moving forward. Furthermore, once a book is analyzed in one locale, it need not be analyzed in another. That is, the results can be shared and used widely, much like crowd-sourcing websites such as Yelp. Finally, this kind of shared work across districts can amplify the potential learning opportunity it offers to teachers.

Another way to reduce the analysis burden is to pick and choose portions of the book to simplify the analysis procedure. A recent investigation found that analyzing just every fifth item (an over 80 percent reduction in analysis burden) resulted in nearly identical results to analyzing the whole book (Polikoff, Zhou & Campbell, in press). It is also possible to analyze just sections of books—say, the section pertaining to fractions—or even independent lessons, and compare those sections with the relevant portions of the standards. The same analysis procedures apply.

Once the analysis is complete, it's time to select a textbook. This is the summative decision resulting from the analysis. It may not necessarily make sense to simply adopt the most-aligned book. Rather, district leaders should take the alignment information into consideration alongside other factors, such as the instructional vision of the district, in making choices.

The utility of the tool does not stop with the selection of a book; indeed, the analysis procedures hold great potential for improving curriculum as well. For one, the results of the analyses can be used to identify gaps in that book that need to be addressed through supplementary materials. For another, the tools can also be used to analyze potential supplementary materials, such as online lessons, to see if they really do fill the gaps.

In the end, the analysis procedure should not be seen merely as an exercise to rate textbooks. The act of analyzing the standards and sets of curriculum materials can be an excellent professional development activity for teachers, particularly if the work is done with a goal of deeply understanding the standards. Focusing in a fine-grained way on the content in the standards can help teachers reflect on the weaknesses and gaps that are invariably present in all curriculum materials, and how teachers will need to improve their instruction and find or create materials to address those weaknesses.

## CONCLUSION

Common standards open the door to improving the quality of curriculum materials and other educational inputs, given the economies of scale that come from sharing materials across schools, districts, and even states. However, many vendors are making bold claims of quality and alignment with relatively little evidence. Some of these claims are undoubtedly true, but many are not. It is no longer enough to take anyone's word about textbook alignment to standards. Educators need to evaluate those claims systematically and rigorously.

This chapter laid out a methodology that can be used by educators in a district to study the alignment of curriculum materials with the Common Core. The Surveys of Enacted Curriculum is not the only approach, but it does have considerable evidence for its feasibility and utility. Similar approaches using simplified frameworks may prove more reasonable for educators, but the key is using a replicable approach that determines alignment in a deep and rigorous way and allows for clear comparisons.

As the curriculum materials market gets savvier, the hope is that quality materials will rise to the top. The kind of work proposed here holds promise for providing the kind of data that could allow districts to make more evidence-based decisions about this important educational input. Furthermore, it holds promise as a teacher development activity. No set of curriculum materials will provide a foolproof way to implement standards in the classroom, but choosing materials more thoughtfully and systematically could go a long way toward easing the transition to new standards and improving student learning on new assessments.

## NOTES

1. For more details on the Surveys of Enacted Curriculum methods, see Porter et al. (2008).

*Chapter Seven*

# Collaborative Professional Development to Create Cognitively Demanding Tasks in English Language Arts

Vivian Mihalakis and Anthony Petrosky

## WHY WE BEGIN BY ENGAGING ADULTS AS LEARNERS IN COGNITIVELY DEMANDING TASKS

People don't learn standards—especially standards like the CCSS that re-quire significantly different and more demanding intellectual work of stu-dents—merely by reading them or by "tracing" or "cross walking" them with other standards. Instead, they learn the expectations of the standards and the pedagogies that enable them by engaging as learners in model lessons or tasks developed from the standards, trying them with students, studying arti-facts of implementation (e.g., student work, classroom video, co-constructed charts), and then developing their own similar lessons or tasks with their colleagues.

Few teachers and leaders have had experiences in their schooling with the kinds of demanding texts, tasks, and supportive pedagogies that the CCSS point educators toward. The mainstays of instruction still reside in teacher talk and teacher questioning of students in a pattern referred to as Initiate, Respond, and Evaluate (I-R-E). The familiar artifacts of these show them-selves in the ways teachers organize and conduct classrooms. They put desks in rows facing the front so that students can listen and talk to the teacher. They call on students to raise their hands one by one, allowing only a few students to answer questions and none to talk with each other. These familiar scenes dominate teaching in ELA/Literacy (Applebee et al., 2003; Goodlad,

2004). In fact, students in most ELA classes have only minutes a year to talk with each other. When students do have opportunities to talk to each other in genuine exchanges of ideas and reasoning, they have higher levels of achievement on standardized tests (Applebee et al., 2003; Guthrie et al., 1995; Langer, 2001; Nystrand & Gamoran, 1997), and find their schooling more fun and engaging (Applebee, 1993; Applebee, Burroughs & Stevens, 1994; Christoph & Nystrand, 2001; Guthrie et al., 1995).

Many of the nation's current teachers and leaders, especially those who entered the profession in the past two decades, have been educated in a system defined by high-stakes, low-quality testing. The heavy-handed emphasis on the testing of No Child Left Behind (NCLB) has resulted in curricula and instruction in which test preparation trumps serious intellectual work (Applebee & Langer, 2013; Darling-Hammond, 2014). Steady diets of this have led people to make the outrageous claim that students cannot handle intellectually challenging work. Multiple-choice and short-answer tests point everyone—students, teachers, and leaders—to instruction that entails reading to regurgitate or identify information or to make low-level inferences drawn from shallow and simple texts.

Writing has fared no better under NCLB. According to the most recent research, the range and length of writing that students are expected to do has fallen off dramatically since the 1980s even for the schools known to have strong writing programs (Applebee & Langer, 2013). Students engage in very little writing that's longer than a paragraph and have limited opportunities to share and discuss their writing with their peers (Applebee & Langer, 2013). Writing instruction, like reading instruction, tends to resemble test preparation rather than intellectual inquiry conducted with cognitively demanding texts, tasks, and supportive pedagogies. Intellectually demanding tasks are rare sightings as well in textbooks, so teachers have few models of what rich texts and text-based tasks look like (Applebee, 1993; Lynch & Evans, 1963; Mihalakis, 2010).

All this means that educators have had few experiences studying and using the kinds of intellectually demanding tasks that should make up the core of CCSS instruction in ELA/Literacy. Considering this, along with what is known about professional learning from the learning sciences, educators can benefit from professional development that anchors their learning in their active engagement in sequences of cognitively demanding tasks that were developed from the standards. This type of active engagement positions educators to understand the standards from the inside out, from direct experiences with the kinds of intellectual work the standards promote.

The benefits of this type of active learning are dramatic. When educators engage with their colleagues in exemplary tasks or lessons developed from clusters of standards, they have a common experiential foundation on which they can develop new knowledge about the standards, about cognitively challenging texts and tasks, and about the types of pedagogies that enable interactive engagement in talk and writing that makes thinking and evidence-based reasoning visible.

At the Institute for Learning (IFL), we use such a collaborative approach in our professional development. IFL fellows provide educators with the following sequence of professional development to help them understand the work and expectations of the standards:

1. Engage teachers as learners in a sequence of cognitively demanding tasks developed from clusters of the CCSS. We structure teachers' engagement so that they experience the demands of the tasks as well as the pedagogy and the talk and writing routines that enable deep engagement with complex texts and cognitively demanding tasks.
2. Invite teachers to reflect on their engagement with their colleagues. We ask them to discuss the content and concepts of the tasks and to identify the pedagogy and routines that guided and shaped their learning. This reflection makes the content and the pathways through it visible and accessible to all participants and helps to transfer professional learning to student learning.
3. Provide a Bridge to Practice assignment that invites teachers to implement the sequence of tasks with their students and to collect artifacts of implementation, such as students' written responses to tasks, recordings of students' discussions, co-constructed class charts, and other products of classroom instruction.
4. Bring teachers together to study artifacts of implementation with their colleagues to determine what students know and can do related to the expectations of the CCSS, and where they need additional instruction. Teachers discuss the pedagogies they used to guide and shape their students' learning, and consider whether their pedagogy maintained or restricted the intellectual demands of the tasks.

After engaging teachers as learners in this sequence, IFL fellows then work collaboratively with teachers to develop their own similar tasks with their colleagues. Before discussing that work, though, a more robust explanation of *cognitively demanding tasks* is in order.

## COGNITIVELY DEMANDING TASKS

Cognitively demanding tasks in ELA/Literacy require students to read, reread, and analyze complex texts to develop oral and written explanations, interpretations, and arguments. These types of tasks are built from complex and worthy texts and focus readers on difficult, interesting, and significant ideas and moments in these texts. They invite rich, extended responses that require students to marshal evidence from across one or more texts. These tasks integrate multiple clusters of standards that reach across reading, writing, speaking and listening, and language, as well as disciplinary best practices.

The following tables present examples of cognitively demanding tasks next to ones that are less demanding. At the IFL, we ask educators to study examples and non-examples as they move from using and analyzing existing tasks to developing new tasks. This is done for several reasons. One has to do with educators' limited experience with these demanding tasks. Another is because it's often the case that tasks that appear at first blush to be intellectually demanding are not. Often tasks are demanding not because of the reasoning that they require but because they are confusing and unfocused. Many sequences of tasks pose loosely related or fuzzy questions that leave students puzzled and unsure how to proceed. Additionally, tasks can often appear demanding because they ask for speculation—sometimes personal or historical or literary or cultural—that reaches beyond the texts and requires knowledge not available to everyone. Providing examples, as well as non-examples, offers everyone in the system a common definition and vision of cognitively demanding tasks while also highlighting the types of tasks that often pass for cognitively demanding.

The English Language Arts Text-Based Task Analysis Guide (table 9.1) provides general criteria for lower-level and higher-level tasks. Educators use this guide to analyze existing tasks and those that they co-develop with the IFL. The chart is divided into comprehension, interpretation, and analysis categories that roughly parallel the ELA/Literacy CCSS anchor standards, but also have their source in a body of research on ELA/Literacy instruction.

The fundamental difference in lower-level and higher-level tasks has to do with how they position readers in relation to texts. The lower-level tasks focus readers primarily on strip-mining texts to find clearly stated ideas, to identify supporting details, and to recognize literary devices. These types of tasks look very much like the multiple-choice and fill-in-the-blank exercises in workbooks and on multiple-choice tests.

The higher-level tasks focus readers on constructing meaning across whole texts. They ask students to track such things as ideas and claims, and they require reasoning that can be supported by marshaling evidence from significant moments across one or more texts. Higher-level tasks invite students to make their reasoning visible in extended, evidence-based discussions and writings, and they are sequenced so that students come away with a coherent understanding of texts. It's also important to note that higher-level tasks demand texts that are rich in ideas and language. It is virtually impossible to develop a sequence of intellectually demanding tasks for a shallow

|  | Lower-Level Demands | Higher-Level Demands |
|---|---|---|
| Comprehension | • Involve finding and identifying information in a text<br>• Can be answered by skimming the text and searching for key words<br>• Invite brief responses<br>• Focus readers' attention on close readings of minor or insignificant details<br>• Ask readers to recall minor details, events, and ideas | • Require close and careful reading to construct meaning from across a complex text<br>• Focus readers' attention on tracking important characters, events, ideas, and claims<br>• Invite multiple entry points and discussion<br>• Invite responses that are articulated in oral and written explanations and arguments<br>• Provide readers with a foundation on which they can build and refine their ideas in subsequent readings |
| Interpretation | • Require speculative thinking or other responses that cannot be anchored in the text<br>• Focus readers' attention on small sections of the text<br>• Take readers away from the text in order to make personal connections or opinions that cannot be supported with textual evidence<br>• Require regurgitating or verifying given interpretations, or choosing between two or three interpretations | • Require close and careful rereading<br>• Require marshaling evidence from across one or more texts to develop oral and written explanations and arguments<br>• Invite multiple and varied responses that can be supported by textual evidence<br>• Focus readers' attention on difficult, interesting, ambiguous, and significant moments in a text or across multiple texts<br>• Invite rich, text-based writing and discussion<br>• Invite extended responses that are articulated in oral and written explanations and arguments |
| Analysis of Craft | • Involve finding and identifying elements in a text<br>• Focus readers' attention on noticing an author's style without making connections to how style shapes meaning<br>• Require speculative thinking, asking readers to state why an author made stylistic choices | • Invite careful study of interesting and significant aspects of an author's style that have broad transferability to other texts, including students' own writing<br>• Focus readers' attention on how an author's style shapes meaning<br>• Invite students to try out the techniques in their own writing<br>• Invite extended responses that are articulated in oral and written explanations and arguments |

**Table 7.1 The English Language Arts Text-Based Task Analysis Guide**

and simplistic text. On the other hand, it is very easy to develop less demanding tasks for a complex text.

Table 9.2 provides examples of lower-level and higher-level cognitively demanding tasks for Martin Luther King's "I Have a Dream" speech. The table indicates the higher-level questions' alignment to the CCSS College and Career Readiness Anchor Standards (CCR) for reading (R), writing (W), and language (L). Questions 11 and 12 also provide examples for the ways students' engagements might play out in a class; as such, these questions are aligned to the speaking and listening (SL) standards as well as the reading, writing, and language standards.

Notice how both lower-level and higher-level tasks ask students to reread or skim texts, but the lower-level tasks often push students back into the text to look for plainly stated answers, to identify ideas or moments, or to regurgi-

| | Lower-Level Demands | Higher-Level Demands |
|---|---|---|
| **Comprehension** | 1. What, according to King, was the "great beacon light of hope"?<br><br>2. What couldn't blacks do in 1963 in Mississippi?<br><br>3. What is King's dream for his four little children? | 8. As you read "I Have a Dream," mark moments that seem important to King's argument. When you're finished reading, look across your marked moments. Then write a sentence or two to capture what you understand King's argument to be. (CCR.R.1)<br><br>9. As you reread "I Have a Dream," pay attention to natural breaks in the speech—places where King transitions to new topics, ideas, or claims. Mark those places. Then, go back and reread each section to try to understand its role in his speech. What is King saying in each section? How does each build from the ones before it and contribute to the text as a whole? (CCR.R.1, 2, 3 & 5) |
| **Interpretation** | 4. Why does King use the word "dream"?<br>5. Do you think King's speech is idealistic or realistic?<br>6. What might your life be like now, if the world had not known MLK? | 10. King refers to freedom and the notion of being free throughout his speech. Draft an essay in which you explain how you think King would define "freedom." What does freedom entail? Draw on evidence from across the speech to support your response. (CCR.R.1, 2 & 4; CCR.W.2, 4 & 9; CCR.L.5)<br>11. What, according to King, is the relationship between freedom and justice? How does brotherhood/sisterhood fit into this relationship? As you reread the speech, locate examples from across the text that you can use to define the relationship of freedom to justice and the place of brotherhood/sisterhood in this relationship.<br><br>When you're finished rereading, compose a quick write in which you answer the question on the relationship of freedom and justice and the ways that brotherhood/sisterhood fit into this relationship. Share and discuss your quick write with a partner. Together, prepare a chart that shows your thinking about these relationships. Use the chart to explain your thinking to the class. (CCR.R.1, 2, 3 & 4; CCR.W.9 & 10; CCR.SL.1 & 4; CCR.L.5) |

**Table 7.2 Sample Tasks Using "I Have a Dream"**

| | | |
|---|---|---|
| **Analysis of Craft** | 7. King uses a fantastic number of metaphors in his speech. Select the two or three that you think are most powerful. Why do you think King uses so many metaphors? | 12. King uses a fantastic number of metaphors in his speech. As you reread, select the two or three that you think are key in advancing King's argument. When you're finished rereading, compose a quick write in which you explain each metaphor and how you think it works to advance King's argument. Share your quick write in trios. Together, prepare a two-column chart. In the left column, write each of King's metaphors followed by your explanation of it in your own words. In the right column, explain how you think each metaphor advances King's argument. Use your chart to explain your thinking to the class. (CCR.R.1, 4 & 5; CCR.W.9 &; CCR.SL.1 & 4; CCR.L.5) |

**Table 7.2 Sample Tasks Using "I Have a Dream" (*cont.*)**

tate known information. The question about what King means by "the great beacon light of hope" (question #1) or "What is King's dream for his four little children?" (question #3) are examples of these types of questions. Such questions ask readers to restate information stated plainly in the text, and the answers are simple restatements rather than extended reasoning.

Several of the lower-level tasks, such as: "What might your life be like now, if the world had not known MLK?" (question #6) and "Why do you think King uses so many metaphors?" (question #7)—ask for speculations. These questions use textual issues as springboards for giving opinions that are not grounded in the text. Such speculations might involve making claims and supporting them with reasoning, but the reasoning will always be quite general since the responses will not be anchored in evidence.

The high-level demand tasks pose questions about difficult concepts such as freedom or the relationship of King's metaphors to his argument. They require that students make claims about their understandings of these concepts from the text, and they ask readers for analyses of the text that involve interpretations based on readers' claims and evidence from across the entire text.

A particularly demanding question, for example, is question #11 from table 9.2. In order to complete this task, students must reread the text, perhaps multiple times, to locate two or three moments that they can use to make and explain claims about the relationship between freedom and justice. Then they need to locate significant moments that they can use to make and explain claims for how King's notions of brotherhood and sisterhood have a role in this relationship between freedom and justice. All of these claims and explanations must be anchored in textual evidence, and the relationship of each piece of evidence to the claims it supports must be explained and argued. Tasks with a high level of cognitive demand such as this one invite students to engage in intellectually demanding work—either in talk or in writing or in both—to warrant claims and make their reasoning and its sources visible.

This task also includes suggestions for the ways students' engagements might play out in a class. Directing students to locate moments in the text, and to use those when they compose a quick write, is a routine that can be used for other tasks and in other situations. The same is true of the directions to compose and share quick writes. Quick writes generate thinking rather than finished writing. As such, they are useful tools for students to see what they are thinking. Sharing these quick writes with a partner encourages evidence-based talk in the fairly safe environment of one or two people working on the same task. Charting makes thinking visible, and when an entire class of students works in pairs and trios, they can all post and share their thinking with charts in preparation for their explanations. The explanations from the charts both help make reasoning visible and can demonstrate ranges of ideas and reasoning, so students learn about fellow students' thinking as well as other ways of using text-based reasoning.

## JUGGLING THE VARIABLES FOR DEVELOPING COGNITIVELY DEMANDING TASKS

Teachers and leaders have a difficult time developing intellectually demanding tasks for students. Lack of experience with these types of tasks is certainly a contributing factor, but more than that, developing these tasks—especially tasks that are sequenced and help students build knowledge about a text or topic—is a difficult and complex process that requires juggling multiple variables at once.

Students' work varies by the challenges presented in the tasks they are asked to do (Matsumura, 2005). Cognitively demanding tasks require texts that present readers with work to do. Furthermore, pedagogies can enable and limit students' interactions in many ways. For example, students can be engaged in challenging tasks with demanding texts yet still have few opportunities to explain their reasoning in talk or in writing when the pedagogy doesn't offer them opportunities to do so. On the other hand, students can be engaged with pedagogies that reflect the types of student-to-student interactions promoted in the CCSS speaking and listening and the writing standards. When they are, they write to understand and express their reasoning, for example, and they talk among themselves to understand, elaborate, and test their reasoning.

When the IFL collaborates with teachers to develop intellectually demanding tasks, one of the first issues fellows address is the relationship among texts, tasks, pedagogies, and standards. All four variables have to work together to support students to build knowledge and to promote learning through social interactions among students. Added to that, the tasks and pedagogies need to make use of appropriate best practices in the discipline. These variables—the affordances and demands of the texts, the tasks, the pedagogies, clusters of standards, and best practices in the discipline—are always at play when creating cognitively challenging tasks. Furthermore, aspects of these variables, such as which clusters of standards to work with or which best practices to use to help students meet the demands of the texts and tasks, change with each new text, since every text affords different kinds of work, resulting in different clusters of standards, tasks, and pedagogies. In other words, there's no template for creating cognitively demanding tasks because texts—and their demands on readers—vary.

Juggling these multiple variables when creating tasks is quite different from the ways educators have created tasks for previous standards. Many educators believe that tasks should align one-to-one with standards. If, for instance, a standard calls for determining central ideas in a text, they design tasks that ask students to underline central ideas in a text or identify central ideas from lists of possibilities. This one-to-one equation for thinking about the relationship of tasks to standards, promoted by the kinds of multiple choice testing done for the high-stakes tests, conflates test preparation with instruction.

The CCSS, on the other hand, promote the types of intellectual engagement that encourage students to talk with their peers and to write about their ideas with text-based reasoning. At the IFL, we support people in creating these kinds of tasks by inviting them to work with clusters of standards that reach across reading, writing, speaking and listening, and language, and by supporting them to think in terms of disciplinary best practices as they've been defined by research in ELA/literacy and in the learning sciences.

Juggling of texts and standards, developing tasks from them, and identifying supportive pedagogies grounded in research on best practices—all while working to sequence texts and tasks to build students' knowledge about a topic—create enormous variability, uncertainty, and at times frustration. Collaboration, though, fuels and sustains the work. Collaboration creates community; it allows people to learn from and with each other, and it offers multiple voices to help think through the various pieces that are in play.

The co-development of tasks always begins slowly and tentatively. Participants read, reread, analyze, and talk about the texts, possible clusters of standards, and possible tasks until they click. Until, that is, they come together in a sequence of tasks that meet the expectations of the standards and adhere to disciplinary best practices while helping students develop a coherent understanding of the text(s) and topic. This co-development is always accomplished through lots of talk and always pushes all participants into new learning about texts, tasks, standards, and best practices. With this collaboration, professional development is a form of socializing intelligence (Resnick & Nelson-LeGall, 1997) for everyone actively participating.

After settling on the tasks in the lessons or units, participants complete the tasks as the first test of whether they work. This almost always results in revisions that can include rewriting tasks, realigning the clusters of standards, or even changing texts. The second test happens when teachers teach the texts and tasks using pedagogies that support students' interactions to make their reasoning visible and collect artifacts of practice. Studying these artifacts almost always signals the need for a second round of revisions.

## THE RESULTS OF COLLABORATIVE DEVELOPMENT

From these collaborative experiences, the educators with whom we work develop as a community of learners. Participants engage in the types of intellectual work highlighted in the CCSS as they talk about text choices in groups of two or three. They make cases for and against particular texts by citing the texts to determine the types of challenges and intellectual work they might offer students. They chart possible sequences of texts. They revise the sequences. They write tasks, always beginning with comprehension questions, and they learn to let the texts tell them the kinds of work to provide. Teachers are taught not to force texts into task templates. When they ask a question such as "What types of work does this text want us to do with it?" they engage as a community of learners in one of the best possible types of close reading, because in order to respond, they have to dig into paragraphs and sentences, they have to find evidence for ideas as well as ambiguities and gaps that invite analysis and interpretation. They anticipate difficulties because they know that each text brings its own affordances and baggage.

Writing challenging and interesting tasks is difficult work. At times, collaborators land on one-sentence questions. Other times, they develop paragraphs-long tasks, such as the ones in the "I Have a Dream" sequence, that provide clear directions along with suggestions for pedagogical approaches in language suited to students. All of this, with all of its variations, takes time, effort, and collaborative sharing. It helps to work in groups of two and three to invite everyone to participate and to encourage intellectual intimacy. Participants critique each other's tasks; they order and reorder them; they rewrite and rewrite until they get as close as they can to having sequences of tasks that both reach across multiple texts and push students deeply, coherently into single texts.

When participants take their development into classrooms and return to the institute with student work samples and notes on their experiences, the group once again turns to the collaborative study and revision prompted by the inevitable differences between what was expected and what actually happened with the taught materials. This cycle of professional development engages us all in exactly the types of intellectual work with texts, with speaking and listening, with language and with writing that the standards ask of students. The trigger for all of it resides in the Institute for Learning's initial collaborative engagement with participants as learners with model lessons IFL fellows created and honed, so that teachers can experience first-hand the intellectual demands of the standards before jumping in to create materials for students.

*Chapter Eight*

# Fulfilling the Promise of Rigor for All

## Emily Hodge

As educators across much of the nation continue to implement the Common Core State Standards (CCSS), how might school and district leaders use the process as an opportunity to create challenging, rigorous, and engaging learning environments that are also *equitable*? In other words, what factors should school and district leaders consider in order to create learning environments in which the knowledge and skills necessary for college readiness are offered to *all students*, not just students in affluent neighborhoods or students who are selected for gifted programs or honors classes? To use the rhetoric of the Common Core, how do schools fulfill the promise of "rigor for all"?

This chapter urges school and district leaders to consider the unintended consequences of two common and interrelated practices that can mute the potential of the CCSS to result in rigor for all. The first is placing a heavy emphasis on test score data. The second is grouping students for instruction into honors and regular classes. Each of these practices can lead to unequal learning experiences, even when conditions for implementing the Common Core seem to be ideal. To illustrate the challenge of equitably enacting the standards, the chapter considers the experiences of Palmetto County Public Schools, a large metropolitan district in the South, as it went through the process of implementing the Common Core standards.[1]

In many ways, Palmetto County is an ideal site for enacting the standards. The district is widely lauded for building consensus and buy-in about the Common Core across different groups of stakeholders over a multiyear period, leaving it less susceptible to the political challenges related to the Common Core in many other contexts. Teachers participated in multiple trainings about the need for, and the major components of, the standards. And the district uses a pre-Advanced Placement curriculum with all middle and high school students, communicating an expectation of rigor for all through uniform exposure to the knowledge and skills necessary for success in Advanced Placement (and, by extension, college) courses.

At the same time, however, Palmetto County places a great deal of emphasis on students' state test score data, using it to group students for instruction and as a data point in evaluating teachers' annual performance. When students are grouped into honors-, advanced-, or regular-level courses based on their state test scores, it can send the signal to teachers that a one-time measure of student performance represents a measure of underlying ability. Responding to these signals, teachers make decisions about how to modify their curriculum and instruction for the lower-level class in ways that do not preserve the rigorous tasks and texts used in the higher-level class.

It's important to note that though this discussion focuses on how these practices were taken up in middle English/Language Arts (ELA) instruction, such practices are common across disciplines and across elementary and secondary schools.

The following sections describe two common factors that can interfere with the potential of the Common Core to create equitably distributed, high-quality learning opportunities. First, I describe how the Common Core interacts with existing policies, particularly the emphasis high-stakes tests. Next, I describe how students are grouped for instruction and the signals that fixed hierarchical instructional grouping sends to teachers. After discussing each of these common factors, the chapter concludes by offering suggestions for how school and district leaders can work within existing policy constraints to support rigor for all.

## HOW AN OVERRELIANCE ON TEST SCORES CAN INFLUENCE TEACHERS' VIEWS OF STUDENTS

The first common practice is to place a heavy emphasis on test score data, especially annual state test scores. While state test score data can provide helpful information about student performance at a global level, an overemphasis on test score data—especially when state test score data are used for instructional grouping—can lead teachers to conflate a one-time measure of student *performance* with student *ability*. Instead of the state test serving as one data point measuring performance at a moment in time, teachers often saw students' state test scores as an accurate way to determine what they viewed as realistic expectations for particular students. Further, because the state test was graded according to five performance levels (1, 2, 3, 4, and 5, with 1 representing the lowest performance level), teachers frequently referred to students by their performance levels.

For instance, when Marcia Johnson,[2] an experienced seventh-grade ELA teacher in a high-income middle school, was asked about the expectations for the quality of student work in her regular-level inclusion class (as opposed to the honors-level class and the regular-level, non-inclusion class), she responded, "I'm lettin' them off a little bit easier, definitely. Definitely. And there are some kids who are in there [the inclusion class] because they have IEPs, but they're a 4, perhaps [on the state test]. . . . So their work has to be better because they can produce the better work." Here, Marcia Johnson demonstrates not only different expectations for students across her different "levels" of classes, but also a connection between students' test scores and their ability: If a student receives a score of 4 on the state test (note the shorthand of a student described as a number), then his or her work must be held to a higher standard of quality.

In addition, teachers frequently described groups of students using the hierarchical, numerical language of the state test. For example, one middle school teacher described her daily schedule:

> I start out with period one, and they are my lower class. They're considered an advanced language arts class, however, they're like the 1s and 2s. . . . And then I go and jump up to an advanced honors class after them, which is language arts as well. They're better writers, better readers. They're my 3s, 4s, a couple of 5s in that class on [the state test]. . . . Then I go to fourth period, which is again an advanced language arts, and these are not as low as the first period, but again, they're like the 2s and maybe some 3s, maybe a couple 1s in there.

Here, this teacher describes her different classes in terms of their state test score distributions, using students' test scores to describe how some classes contain "better writers" and "better readers" than those classes that are "lower" or "not as low as the first period."

In addition to using state test score data to describe groups of students, teachers sometimes conflated students' state test scores with students themselves, as in a lesson I observed whose goal was to prepare students for the state writing test. In this lesson, students were asked to look at examples of student writing the state had released to illustrate the characteristics of essays that receive of a score of 1 or 2, and so on, all the way up to the top score of 6. As the teacher transitioned from one scoring level to the next, his refrain was, for example, "Let's look at a 2 [i.e., an essay that received a score of 2]. What are 2s doing better than 1s?" Obviously, an essay did not "do anything better" than another essay, so the conflation here was between the student who had written the essay and the level at which the essay had been scored.

A similar example occurred just a bit later in the lesson, when students looked at an example of an essay receiving a score of 3. The teacher said to the honors-level class, "So you can see they [the student whose essay had a score of 3] have a little idea of how to write . . . small and minute . . . but they do know how to write better than those 1s and 2s." Similar language occurred the entire day, in which the essay scores were personified and conflated with the students who wrote the essay.

While on the one hand, this language of 1s, 2s, 3s, 4s, and 5s provides convenient shorthand for teachers to describe the overall performance level of groups of students, these examples also demonstrate how easily this shorthand can become the dominant language that teachers use with each other to describe students, as well as the dominant language that teachers use with students to describe their performance in reductive ways. Personifying data points in classroom instruction—as in the example above about how to write a high-scoring essay on the state test, so that students are conflated with their test scores—can send the message to students that their teachers think of them as test scores.

On the other hand, teachers can use test score data in more positive ways that signal to students that their performance is just that—one snapshot of their performance. When teachers talk about students' test scores without talking about students *as* test scores, it much more clearly communicates to both adults and students that test performance is one data point—and a mutable one. For example, a writing coach assigned to a low-performing middle school described telling students who had scored at a level 1 or 2 on the previous year's test:

> "This is unacceptable. If you're writing at a 1 or 2 right now, there's no reason, if you follow what I've been teaching you." I show them samples of a 1 or 2. . . . I'm like, "If this is a 1 or 2 and you're telling me this is the best you can do, you're lying to yourself, to me. This is something where you have the opportunity to show the state, show yourself, show us that you are a good writer." I have to tell them, "It's not hard, but you have to apply yourself, and you have to want it."

Not only does this writing coach use numbers to describe *performance* rather than to describe a student, she also emphasizes that the score is not fixed. Rather, it is mutable based on students' effort and willingness to work with the coach.

Another example comes from Lisa Cooper, a sixth- and eighth-grade teacher in a low-income school, whose students found the adjustment from the former state test (emphasizing narrative writing) to the new Common Core practice tests (emphasizing argumentative writing) to be difficult. Lisa Cooper used the first practice writing test at the beginning of the year to set goals. She emphasized that this was a pretest situation, in which students were being asked to do something that she hadn't taught them how to do yet:

> I gave the kids back their essays, and when they saw 1s, and these are kids who are used to getting 5s and 6s. . . . They were like, "Oh, my gosh! I suck! What is this?" I had a couple kids in tears. I said, "Don't freak out. Here's the good

news. Yeah, this was hard. Everyone did bad. In fact, in this class not a single person passed. But here's the good news. Now I know exactly where you're at, and now I know where we can go from here. This is where we'll start. We'll talk about unpacking a prompt. This is how you unpack the prompt. You need to know what you're being asked to write about. How many of you understood the prompt?"... And we took the next step. "Now let's talk about planning."

Like the writing coach described above, Lisa Cooper used numbers to describe students' *performance* rather than students themselves, and as she returned the diagnostic essays, she immediately began to model the steps students should follow to be able to write a successful essay for a Common Core-style state assessment.

## THE UNINTENDED CONSEQUENCES OF INSTRUCTIONAL GROUPING

When heavy emphasis is placed on students' state test scores, and those test scores are also used to group students for instruction into advanced honors, advanced, and regular levels of a particular course, this practice can send messages to teachers that students are not capable of reading or engaging in the same text. Teachers then adjust their instruction accordingly. Often, these decisions are based on good intentions—teachers' desire to match curriculum and instruction to what they perceive as the appropriate needs of their students. Here, I offer an alternative approach that preserves rigor for all, but that varies the level of instructional support and scaffolding rather than instructional task.

Many teachers across Palmetto County modified aspects of their curriculum and instruction to meet their assessment of students' needs across the different levels of English/Language Arts they taught. One way that teachers sometimes modified the curriculum to match their assessment of what different groups of students needed was by making choices about which texts to use with different groups of students. Multiple teachers expressed the feeling that some of the texts in the pre-Advanced Placement curriculum were unrealistic for students in the lower-level class to comprehend. One eighth-grade teacher, April Martin, felt that the excerpt from Sir Thomas More's *Utopia*—with its long, convoluted sentences and sophisticated vocabulary—was too difficult for students in the lower-level class. Similarly, another eighth-grade teacher, John Maxwell, felt that even beyond the convoluted syntax, comprehending the *Utopia* excerpt required a level of background knowledge that all of his students—but particularly his "lowest readers"—just do not possess. In response, teachers would often skip texts like these, or read them aloud to students.

One example comes from John Maxwell, who described his instruction around an excerpt from *The Odyssey* in the lower-track class as "a lot more teacher-directed." In his words,

> In my honors class I can say, "All right, read it. It's gonna be tough. It's gonna be difficult, but you can get through it. Mark the text. We're lookin' for problems and solutions." They're gonna struggle a little bit because Homer's complex for an eighth grader to understand. With my regular kids, it was more, "All right, I'm gonna read it," [laughs] because I know if I say, "Read eight pages," they're gonna just sit there and they're not gonna read it, because they don't even have the reading level to be able to make a little bit of meaning from the text. So I read it out loud, and then I'm kind of modeling. "This is a problem." We work together. . . . You've read Homer, I'm sure. It's preposi-tional phrases modifying prepositional phrase modifying—and low-level read-ers, they don't get that it's just saying, "We fought for Agamemnon." It's "We fought for Agamemnon, son of this, destroyer of this," and by the time they get to the end of the sentence, they're like, "I don't even know what this says anymore." So for me, I have my ELMO [overhead projector] and I put the text under the ELMO and we read it and they followed along . . . [and then periodically I say] Let's stop. Is this a problem to Odysseus and his men? Yeah, that's a problem. Let's put a P next to it." Modeling what good readers do, because they have very few strategies when it comes to reading, and that's why they struggle a lot of times at school.

Here, John Maxwell describes allowing students in his honors-level class to read the text independently and take notes on the problem and solution described in *The Odyssey* excerpt. His rationale for this approach is that students placed in the honors class have the reading comprehension to come to a basic understanding of *The Odyssey* excerpt and can be coached to persist through a difficult text. In the class for the "regular kids," John Max-well chose to read the text aloud *to* students and take a "more teacher-dirccted" approach to meet his assessment of students' needs. While model-ing reading strategies is certainly a helpful form of instructional scaffolding, reading the entire passage to students in the lower-level class does not build students' capacity to comprehend difficult texts independently.

In contrast to John Maxwell's approach, Lisa Cooper supplemented *The Odyssey* excerpt with other resources that help students understand the plot in her eighth-grade ELA class for English language learners. Lisa Cooper provided background information in a visual format to assist with students' comprehension (for example, a clip from the History Channel retelling the story of Odysseus and the Cyclops). She also used the video to help students clarify unfamiliar words in the text (such as *entrails*), as well as to repeatedly expose students to the text in different genres, so that all students could access the meaning of the text regardless of their current level of English proficiency. In her description:

> I said to them [her class of English language learners], "Look, some of the teachers just skip over it [*The Odyssey*] because they think it's too difficult. What do you guys think?" And they were like, "We want to do it." I said, "All right, but we have to break it apart, we have to look at language, we have to look at history." Because the kids have no knowledge of Greek mythology. We started working on it at the beginning of the week, and I just showed them the video clip from the History Channel that covers some of the details, and we did what we call a fusing, which is a vocabulary strategy where as you're reading, and we do mostly shared readings, you circle the words and then you have dialogue, in groups or as a whole class, with, "Can you determine the meaning of the word based on context clues? If you can't, here's a Spanish-English dictionary, let's figure it out."

After reading the excerpt, students engaged with the theme of the unit, which was defining a hero. Based on *The Odyssey* excerpt, students were to "write an analytical paragraph using textual evidence to reinforce the idea that Odysseus is an epic hero." To make sure that her instruction would enable her English language learners to succeed on that task, Lisa Cooper described how she had students brainstorm four qualities of a hero, "including fearless, faithful, mentally strong, smart," and then watch the video clip multiple times. As they watched the video, students looked for examples of those qualities,

> and then we went to the text and picked out specific evidence, wrote down which page number, because we also labeled the paragraph, there were, like, twenty-seven paragraphs, which paragraph, so that when they write their analytical piece tomorrow, they can go back and say, "If I'm gonna write about him being brave, I can go to this page, this paragraph, and that's where I'll find the information."

There are multiple ways to interpret each of the examples above, and there is legitimate debate in English/language arts and literacy about what the Common Core State Standards mean for classroom instruction (see, for example, Hodge & Benko, 2014). Lisa Cooper began instruction for her English language learner students around *The Odyssey* by showing a video clip of the relevant portion. Some would argue that it is more "Common Core-ish" (as teachers said in my research site) to compare and contrast multiple representations of the same text; yet, Lisa Cooper engaged students in not just comprehension of text well beyond their independent reading level, but also engaged them in using textual evidence to make a point about the text—a sophisticated practice that is equally "Common Core-ish." On the other hand, John Maxwell used the high-leverage practice of modeling as he read the text to students so that they could understand how a skilled reader would interact with the text. However, the key difference between John Maxwell and Lisa Cooper was their underlying assumption about students' ability to

engage with such texts and tasks. Unlike John Maxwell, Lisa Cooper assumed that students would be able to comprehend the *same* text and complete the *same* task as students in the higher levels of ELA.

## HOW SCHOOL LEADERS CAN SUPPORT RIGOR FOR ALL

Given our current policy context, in which an emphasis on test scores and
common attitudes about differentiation can constrain the "rigor for all" rhetoric of the CCSS, what can district and school leaders do to realize the potential of rigor for all?

While district leaders cannot control state policy, they *can* carefully consider the instructional groupings that are mandated and/or encouraged at the
district level. For example, some states require remedial reading instruction
for students who do not pass the state reading test, but that does not mean
that students need to be grouped by state test score in English/Language Arts
classes as well. There are numerous examples of schools that offer a reduced
or single-track curriculum, using advisory periods and other supports built
into the school day so that the instructional rigor of courses does not diminish.

In addition, district leaders should carefully consider the criteria upon
which instructional groupings are made. Grouping students primarily by the
single, outdated data point of the prior year's test score, with little flexibility
to move students from one level to the next, is not the kind of grouping
practice that educational research supports. It is difficult *not* to emphasize
state test scores when they are a critical data point for school grades and
teacher evaluations. However, just as leaders create the policy conditions that
can influence teachers to see student ability as hierarchical and fixed, leaders
can create the policy conditions that help teachers to see student ability as
mutable.

Both school and district leaders can encourage and build the capacity of
their teachers around instructional scaffolding and encourage a mutable view
of student ability, in which teachers are encouraged to use student performance data as a guide for the kind of instructional scaffolding that may be
necessary to enable students at all readiness levels access to the *same* texts
and the *same* tasks, with a similar level of quality in the final product. A
common curriculum is not a guard against different expectations, however.
As the research described above indicates, teachers using a common curriculum sometimes skip texts they think are too difficult and have lower requirements for the quality of student work in the lower-level class.

When policies like the CCSS imply that all students are capable of complex work, but other policies, like instructional grouping via state test score,
imply that all students may not be capable of complex work, the end result is

a set of mixed signals sent to teachers about student ability. These mixed signals influence the potential of the CCSS, or any other instructional reform, to work toward greater equity.

Though school leaders and district officials cannot wave a magic wand and eliminate state tests or the consequences placed on state tests by state and/or federal laws, they *can* support teachers in developing a view of all students as *able* to access the same kinds of instructional experiences and produce work with a high degree of quality. Further, school and district leaders can increase teachers' knowledge of instructional scaffolding so that they are able to make "rigor for all" a reality for all of the students in their classrooms.

## NOTES

1. Palmetto County is a pseudonym.
2. All names used here are pseudonyms.

*Chapter Nine*

# Common Core in Uncommon Schools

*Tools to Strengthen Teacher Collaboration?*

Bruce Fuller

The Common Core—aiming to energize teachers and lift students—will take root in varying terrain across the nation's array of uncommon schools. Its designers hope to deliver a neatly packaged yet complex bundle of learning aims and ways of engaging students, promising to enliven classrooms. Yet as a pedagogical tool kit, the Core will be graphed onto the practices and classroom scripts of diverse teachers situated among a kaleidoscope of local schools and communities. The recurrent yearning for *common-ness* or *uniformity* across America's classrooms runs headlong into the organizational diversity engineered by many of the same reformers now so enthused over the Common Core.[1]

The Core's architects build from virtuous tenets: All students must be challenged by tasks that yield complex learning and reasoning skills, motivated by thicker conversation in classrooms. Yet teachers hold bedrock principles as well, increasingly tied to the curricular mission or pedagogy of the expanding range of charter, magnet, site-managed, or mission-driven campuses. Only the Core's faithful believe that dictated proficiencies or standard pedagogies will come to be held in common, the metaphorical apple core inside schools. Instead, teachers first build from the particular mission held by their comrades, whether dedicated to basic skills, theater arts, dual-language immersion, STEM (science, technology, engineering, mathematics), or social justice. Consider, for example, the New York high school that integrates a dazzling rainbow of teens around the study of animal care. Like the aspiring veterinarians at this school, almost a third of the nation's students no longer attend their garden-variety neighborhood school. Even the common

91

metaphor for these schools is now stigmatized, connoting a campus without coherence, pitching no curricular shtick.[2]

I worry that the Core's designers place teachers on the receiving end of yet another well-meaning reform, unaware or unconcerned that their complicated package of behavioral and intellectual expectations, aligned texts, and new tests now alight on a diversifying array of schools. The Core's architects run the risk of spurring collective resistance inside schools rather than offering robust, yet flexible, tools that spark collaboration, a shared spirit of deeper learning, and new ways of engaging students. After a generation of standards-based accountability, teachers have read the incentives all too well: teach to what's tested. As one inspiring history teacher in Boston recently quipped, "I don't pay much attention [to the Core], I don't teach a tested subject."

This chapter offers a tandem message. First, the Common Core will be interpreted, adapted, even resisted by a breathless diversity of teachers located in varying kinds of schools, often advancing a particular mission or rallying behind a certain pedagogical strategy. Second, unless district and school leaders see the Core as a fungible set of tools—not a tightly aligned doctrine enforced via uniform methods—teachers will struggle to blend the Core's vibrant learning aims and engaging pedagogies into everyday practice.

This chapter urges readers to consider how the Core's tool kit—if forged and wielded *collaboratively* within schools—may well inspire deeper learning by teachers and students alike. The Core asks teachers to reverse much of what the policy apparatus has demanded of them over the past generation. If the ambitious learning aims and participatory pedagogy promoted by the Core are taken to heart only by already inventive teachers or lone artisans, it will fail to stir richer conversation among teachers inside their local contexts. This chapter highlights what's being learned about social cohesion and collaboration inside schools, as teachers rally around their local, often idiomatic commitments. By ignoring the particulars of school context, the Core's enthusiasts risk sparking a shared skepticism rather than a collective embrace.

## THE WIDENING DIVERSITY OF UNCOMMON SCHOOLS

The Common Core lands in a breathtaking diversity of uncommon schools— local organizations that sport a variety of curricular missions, pedagogical strategies, and colorful students. For all the policy talk of standards, commonality, and accountability, policy leaders have spurred the creation of diversifying forms of schooling. Magnet schools, set on integrating children since the 1970s, continue to grow: over 2.3 million students were enrolled by 2009, and the number of magnet students now exceeds the count of pupils attending charter schools. New York City's Education Options Program brings together students across racial and social-class bounds within 347 mission-driven programs inside traditional schools. Miami-Dade has expanded pupil enrollments in their magnet offerings by almost half over the past 3 years.

The count of charter schools continues to climb at 11 percent annually, while serving 4 percent of all students nationwide. The number of students attending charters rose from about 350,000 in 1999 to just over two million in 2011. Three fifths (59 percent) of all charter students attend campuses situated in seven states: Arizona, California, Florida, Michigan, New York, Ohio, and Texas. In several cities—including Dayton, Detroit, Indianapolis, New Orleans, and Philadelphia—over one-third of all students now attend charter schools.

A variety of small and site-managed high schools have proliferated over the past decade as well. Former New York mayor Michael Bloomberg led the controversial charge to close down huge high schools and then create over 320 small campuses over the past decade. The Los Angeles school district imported the pilot school model from Boston, opening fifty-one semi-autonomous pilots by 2014. This model explicitly invites mission-led pedagogies, from art and design, to digital design or social justice themes.

Many pilot schools are created by reform-minded teachers, eager to remain within district-wide salary schedules and pension systems while shaking free of centralized instructional regimes and staffing and budget rules (Fuller, 2010). These teachers report a keen desire to craft stronger methods of engaging and motivating urban students—not unlike their inventive cousins in charter or magnet schools—by setting demanding expectations while moving away from delivery of static knowledge or quickly tested proficiencies.

The Common Core now lands among this medley of increasingly diverse organizations in which teachers labor amid uneven levels and forms of collaboration and varying ways of engaging their students.

## THE COMMON CORE ENTERS COMPLEX SCHOOLS

This ambitious reform pushes for unprecedented complexity in the learning objectives and pedagogical agility demanded of teachers. The intervention doesn't simply ask educators to tack on tutoring for poor readers, harp on phonemes, or study test results. The Core presses complicated learning tasks to advance intricate cognition, furthered by expecting students to verbalize how they are thinking and what questions come into their minds. This curricular and pedagogical reform requires that teachers learn how to *work together*, aligning learning aims across subjects and grade levels.

Two particular elements of the multifaceted Core will necessitate a wild variety of local adaptations among schools, depending on their own mission and educational tenets, not to mention the variability in pupils served.

First, the Common Core advances a range of *complex learning and social objectives*, especially in language arts and math. The aim is to shift "the focus of literacy instruction to center on careful examination of the text itself . . . on students reading closely to draw evidence and knowledge from the text" (Coleman & Pimental, 2012). Or, rather than memorizing procedures for adding fractions, children must now reason through the mathematical concept and verbalize their thinking, even their "meta-cognition" in how they reflect on their mental process (Wu, 2011). Just what are they thinking? What questions, previously unspoken, come into their minds? The growing presence of English learners requires that home language be respected and scaffolded to advance literacy *and* mathematics proficiencies.[3] Teachers must interpret the Core's intent with regard to such challenges, and then integrate these robust aims into their everyday practice.

The second element of the Core stems from how its architects assume that such complexities—both the range of cognitive engagements and agility of social interactions inside classrooms—will sprout with only slight customization by teachers. Well-meaning scholars even seek to associate unfettered installation of Common Core with higher student achievement, ignoring the variable guts and culture of local school organizations (Schmidt & Houang, 2012).

Yet the Core's learning aims and pedagogical methods require innovative and steady *social action* by teachers and students, who must now conceive of knowledge and cognitive prowess as stemming from the verbalizing ideas and feelings. And the alignment of objectives across subject areas and grade levels can only occur with thicker conversations and cooperative work among teachers inside school organizations. It's difficult to imagine a pedagogical revolution of this complexity taking root in the hearts and minds of isolated teachers—each making idiosyncratic sense of the Core while sealed off in their own classrooms. But the Core's architects hardly recognize how all this social innovation is so intertwined with the culture and habits of school organizations.

A half century of research and experience details how richer relationships among teachers often yield technical and social benefits that help to lift students. One study that followed Chicago teachers over two decades found that staff displaying greater trust and shared commitment to lifting students did, in fact, boost test scores and teacher motivation (Bryk et al., 2010). Such discoveries keep recurring, starting with early efforts to restructure schools, followed by a succession of interventions meant to liberate teachers from their own classrooms so that they can nurture deeper relationships and synchronize practices with their colleagues school-wide.

Research inside small Los Angeles high schools—both charters and labor-friendly, site-managed pilot schools—similarly reveals much stronger levels of trust in and respect for colleagues, a collective spirit that energizes collaboration and richer ties with students, compared with large comprehensive high schools (Fuller et al., 2014). These diverse, human-scale schools also build from their own core principles: getting to know each student, curricular aims tied to pupil-crafted projects, evening performances, or building from children's bilingual skills and cultural knowledge. In short, the fine-grained cognitive or social proficiencies embedded in the Core might be best situated within a school's particular mission, as a teacher-crafted strategy through which their colleagues and students feel efficacious and energized about their daily work.

## HOW COMMON TOOLS COULD UNIFY TEACHERS

Across the nation's diverse schools and neighborhoods, what pedagogical and social-organizational tools arriving with the Core might animate closer collaboration among teachers? How might the common features of the Common Core—potentially durable classroom tools sprinkled across the land—help to build more coherent social communities inside uncommon schools?

### Rethinking the Teacher's Role

The new complexity of learning proficiencies advanced by the Core might usefully shake the teacher's traditional role—moving away from the lone professional honing her craft inside her own classroom. Getting up to speed on the Core's content and implied cognitive proficiencies will no doubt focus attention on the teacher's own knowledge and individual skills inside the classroom. But aligning these aims, methods, and pedagogical innovations requires *social action* among teachers, and also requires a rethinking of the core tasks of teachers' school-wide roles. Or consider early complaints by some parents that they don't understand the Core's math problems or that the questions put to literature feel so complicated. These pressures will further press teachers to rethink the mix of daily activities, engaging pupils and a variety of adults.

The Core aims to enliven conversations with and among students, whether digging into how kids are confused or the questions that sprout from their own readings. This, too, requires that teachers connect around how they engage students and how to better collaborate on more agile pedagogical practices. Inventive charter schools often emphasize project-based learning and helping students construct customized portfolios of challenging activities and products, from architectural designs to family histories, as well as a stronger focus on pupils' own emerging identities and interests (Fuller &

Parker, in press). Complex cognitive or collaborative skills can be nurtured via such methods. This may combat the tendency of teachers (as with other artisans) to drift back into established, if uninspired, routines.

## Nurturing Teacher Networks, Coaching Each Other

Teachers naturally chat about—celebrate or wring their hands over—the Common Core. While curriculum designers and district managers obsess over the formalities of delivering training or new textbooks, teachers' informal conversations and shared struggles may prove more telling for how the Core is variegated and planted in local soil. We know that social networks evolve among teachers, often anchored by authoritative teacher-leaders working to strengthen or subvert a school's traditional organizational chart. Teachers come together in hallways and lunchrooms to talk about a feisty student, pedagogical ideas, where to meet for a beer at day's end.[4]

These informal networks come together based on personal attributes of teachers and grade or subject-matter loyalties. Such ties stem from leadership roles and task groups structured by principals. Indeed, teacher-leaders and principals may talk up the Core's tools within official committees inside schools, or via the informal ties and circles that often exert the real power. Principals, eager to wield the Core's new tools, might attend to these teacher networks, which will come to embrace or undercut selected features of this imported reform.

## Building Organizational Capacity School-Wide

The learning expectations and novel forms of pedagogy pressed by the Core will only work if viewed as a social initiative, not one in which teachers as experts ramp-up in isolation of one another. The technocratic conception of how to make learning aims and pedagogy more uniform—witness the didactic "teacher-proof" texts and teaching guides spawned under No Child Left Behind—cast the spotlight on the individual skills of teachers and discrete pieces of curriculum enshrined in state standards. Enriching the individual's knowledge or practice, of course, remains pivotal—be it the observed competencies of teachers or the testable bits and pieces held inside the student's head.

Still, the Core aims to change this mindset, pitching complex knowledge conveyed through social tasks, motivating interactions between teacher and pupil, or among students engaged with content *and* each other. It's difficult to see how such social innovations will take root inside classrooms without richer collaboration and inventive social action among teachers. So, the durable implementation of the Core will necessarily be conditioned by the school's long-term capacity to host serious conversation among teachers.

All this implies discernible change in the social organization of the school: more and mindfully arranged time to work together; smaller and personally attentive settings for teachers and pupils alike; careful articulation of learning aims and pedagogical innovations across subject areas and grade levels. And again, these school-wide shifts will look different, conditioned by a school's own mission, whether it swivels on performing arts, dual language in Mandarin, digital technology, or animal care.

Individualistic conceptions of re-skilling the teacher or the isolated competencies of the lone child will continue to push into schools. Take, for instance, Washington's recent insistence that teachers be observed with pedagogical checklists in hand, or the recasting of standardized testing to gauge pupils' absorption of the Core's learning aims. It's not that these efforts are misguided; it's that they distract from the *collaborative* social change that's required for teachers to rally around the Core's well-intentioned tools. For if these tools are not forged and bent for local contexts *in concert with fellow teachers*, the Core will face the fate of a half-century of outside intrusions that have come before it, too often lacking the invitation for teachers to wield novel tools to craft their practice with fellow professionals.

Instead, the Core could spur sustained efforts to build the organizational capacity of schools to experiment with pedagogies, to examine deeper, more meaningful ways to connect with students. To take just one example, researchers have documented how some charter schools—led by agile principals and teacher-leaders—have pressed forward on inventive pedagogies and caring ways of scaffolding up from pupils' own interests (Fuller, in press). Some forward-thinking charter-management organizations have reshaped how time is used, encouraging richer conversation among teachers, pitching the inventive use of cross-subject projects, debates, evening performances, or portfolio development to advance complex cognitive and cooperative social skills.

## Resisting Test-Driven Pedagogy and Student Growth

Researchers studying collaboration inside small L.A. high schools discovered that teachers spend considerable time talking about students. The rise of richer data on kids' learning curves may offer additional insight into their growth. The point is that teachers are constantly gauging how students are doing, whether acquiring expected skills or making friends on the playground. This key chatter may form the foundation for teacher relationships as well, providing the grist for social networks that variably bind teachers to one another.

So, the arrival of new tests aligned with the Core's robust learning aims will be weighed by teachers who already talk much about their students and the snags limiting their development. Teachers will certainly zero in on the proficiencies highlighted in these standardized exams; they will circulate pirated questions; some will be asked to spend weeks on test prep. Here, too, the utility of testing data will offer grist for teachers to collaborate—either to collectively discern those skills that require more work, or to unite in opposition to the Core's ambitious expectations. Again, it's not that teachers fail to notice and discuss how different students are doing. The question is whether the data stemming from new tests will help teachers adjust their pedagogy, attending to wider and deeper pupil competencies. And will the Core's renewed faith in standardized testing yield data and tools that rally teachers to work together, or simply breed a shared skepticism of this intervention arriving from the sky high above?

## TOGETHER, BRINGING COMMON CORE TO LIFE

The major takeaways of this chapter are as follows: Whether or not this far-reaching reform sinks roots into local schools will be conditioned by the *particular mission* and the *professional coherence* enacted by teachers inside. The Core's authors may hope that it will be adopted with fidelity by schools across the country, like uniform seeds spread across the land, yielding standard fruit. In reality (I promise to wind down this metaphor) the fruit borne of the Common Core will resemble heirloom varieties of differing shapes and flavors, as plentiful and varied as if strolling through a bustling farmers' market. The commonalities intended by its designers will ironically be subverted by the organizational riot of charter, magnet, pilot, and deregulated site-run schools earlier pitched by many of the same reformers who now press the Common Core.

Second, the repertoire of tools offered by the Core—shared learning aims, pedagogies that nudge reasoning and complex thinking, along with vocal and lateral conversations now required in classrooms—may spark rich collaboration among teachers. We know that students benefit most when teachers coordinate learning aims across subject areas and grade levels, when they express a shared responsibility and trust in each another for lifting all pupils.

Yet this requires a sustained shift in the character of school organizations, as detailed above: (1) rethinking the teacher's role as pedagogical innovator and one who connects deeply with students; (2) nurturing networks of teachers within schools that advance the Core's demanding learning aims and inventive pedagogies; (3) building organizational capacity, restructuring time, and structuring collaborative time and tasks that teachers find motivating; and (4) resisting test-driven pedagogy and remaining honest to the complex and participatory forms of learning intended by the Core's hopeful materials, even when the new exam regimen threatens the balance between knowledge mastery and agile social engagement inside classrooms.

As yet another reform arrives from the outside, school leaders are being asked to muster the collective will to make it work. But unless policymakers and local educators recognize the diversity of schools in which the Core now lands, and then press to enhance organization-wide capacity and teacher collaboration, this worthy reform will likely flounder.

## NOTES

1. Portions of the original research for this chapter were conducted with Celina Lee Chao and Anisah Waite, and funded by the Spencer Foundation.

2. Details and sources regarding the widening range of diverse schools and parental choice appear in Fuller, Dauter, & Waite (in press). New roles for teachers in diverse schools. In C. Bell and D. Gitomer (eds.), *Handbook of research on teaching, 2015.* New York: Routledge and American Educational Research Association.

3. For review of how teachers are trying to integrate Common Core math standards into classrooms dominated by English learners, see Rebora, A. (2014). Math standards put new focus on English-learners. *Education Week*, November 12, S12, S15.

4. For review of work on teacher networks, see Daly, A. (ed.) (2010). *Social network theory and educational change.* Cambridge, MA: Harvard Education Press.

*Part 3 Introduction*

# Building System Capacity through Relationships

## James P. Spillane

The three chapters in this section examine the critical role of the broader educational improvement ecosystem of resources that can help leaders to develop their system capacities to respond more productively to the CCSS. These chapters offer a vision of the broader education landscape (made up of both system and non-system actors) that is largely incoherent, fragmented, and often driven by fads. Most importantly, these chapters underscore the ways in which schools and school districts are the key agents for both tapping into and fending off the larger milieu through selective interactions and partnerships.

In chapter 10, Thomas Hatch of Teachers College at Columbia University argues for more sophisticated thinking about alignment that moves beyond simply aligning the elements of school systems to enabling and supporting coherence in the ways people are thinking and acting around instruction. Hatch contends that the fixation with alignment in school systems misses the essence of the challenge that is coherence. Specifically, how can school systems be redesigned so that they provide schools and school districts with environments that have coherent vision for instruction and its improvement? At the core of this chapter is the need to create structures (e.g., standards, assessments, professional development) that are not simply aligned with one another but that together create coherent opportunities and incentives for school and school system staff to develop shared understandings of instruction that lead to better instructional practices.

In chapter 11, Donald Peurach of the University of Michigan makes the case for a shift in how educators think about engaging with our environment in order to build the necessary capacity to meet the challenge of standards. Peurach argues that rather than thinking about capacity as something that is out there that can be imported whole cloth into their organization, educators need a new mindset for thinking about capacity and how best to build it more sustainably through ongoing collaboration with external agents and agencies. Educators' faith in useful external expertise that is fully formed and off-the-rack is overly optimistic. Rather, educators need to think more about partnering smartly with external agents and agencies so that they can tailor capacity to their particular needs. Even more importantly, this allows for schools and districts to tap into external organizations, not only for services but to help them build their own sustainable capacity. The chapter sketches key things to consider as education organizations pursue a partner in the vast education marketplace.

In chapter 12, Patricia Burch of the University of Southern California and her colleagues Andrew LaFave and Annalee Good focus on the new frontier of online resources for CCSS enactment. They consider the potential offered by these new digital resources and underscore the obligation of the local consumer to understand and ask tough questions about the utility and demands of digital products that go beyond the hype of their promoters. The authors press the educators who are consumers in this new market not to accept the label "CCSS aligned" at face value and to inquire as to whether the tools and services actually meet the specific needs of their particular student population. Further, they encourage consumers to critically examine whether and how the digital tools and services allow for customization in order to support individual student needs and particular subpopulations of students.

Here are several questions and points for you and your colleagues to discuss to better build system capacity through relationships:

1. Based on your reading of chapter 10, how have your notions about alignment changed? Identify three dimensions that a coherence framework brings to the fore that are missed in an alignment framework.
2. List who you are currently partnering with to support CCSS implementation. Pick any two and analyze the relationships with each against the dimensions identified in chapter 11 by Peurach.
3. Consider your current investment in digital resources. Identify a key investment that you think is critical to CCSS implementation. Based on your reading of chapter 12, critically analyze whether and how these tools and services allow for customization to your particular student population and subpopulations.

## Chapter Ten

# Connections, Coherence, and Common Understanding in the Common Core

## Thomas Hatch

The Common Core presents educators with a learning problem, not an implementation problem. In other words, determining how to put in place, on a broad scale, solutions that have already been proven to work is not the real challenge. The real challenge lies in learning from what's working and what isn't in order to reach goals that have never been reached before (Supovitz & Spillane, this volume).

Approaching the Common Core as a learning problem rather than as an implementation program depends on a fundamental shift in mindset. It means shifting from seeing the implementation of the Common Core as a goal in itself to viewing the Common Core as providing tools, resources, constraints, and opportunities that educators can use to help them reach higher standards for all students. Obviously, taking advantage of these constraints and opportunities demands significant capacity building throughout the education system.

But what, exactly, does capacity building involve? Conventional notions of capacity building focus on the amount of money and resources (often referred to as "technical capital") needed to reach a particular goal (Newmann, King & Youngs, 2000). The evaluations of the systemic and state-level reform efforts in the 1990s, however, make it clear that money and resources alone are not sufficient to produce large-scale improvements in learning. In contrast, emerging conceptions of capacity building also highlight the importance of developing the knowledge, skills, and motivation— the "human capital"—that enable people to use money and resources productively. These new conceptions of capacity building also emphasize establish-

ing the relationships, trust, and collective commitment—the "social capital"—that enable people and groups to work together effectively.

While many improvement efforts focus on building capacity *inside*
schools, reaching higher standards for all also depends crucially on building
technical, human, and social capital *outside* schools. Schools depend on a
host of people, organizations, and institutions to produce the funding, facil-
ities, technologies, tools, textbooks, and other materials that create productive conditions for learning. The skills and abilities of school staff depend on
the quality and effectiveness of teacher preparation and leadership programs,
the availability of high-quality professional development programs, and the
support of informed and knowledgeable higher-education faculty members,
researchers, and policymakers. Ultimately, the coordination and effectiveness of the work of all those involved in education also depend on the
development of relationships and social networks that build connections
among those in schools and districts and among all those people and organizations involved in the educational enterprise (see figure 10.1) (Hatch,
2013).

Work on the Common Core takes into account the need to develop technical and human capital by seeking to catalyze the creation of Common
Core–aligned learning materials and professional development, as well as
preparation programs that can support teachers' and students' work in the
classroom. But, to date, the implementation of the Common Core largely
ignores the need for social capital and the development of productive relationships and social networks among individuals, groups, and organizations.
This chapter[1] describes some of the mechanisms and activities that support
and inhibit the development of social networks at the system and district
levels, and recommends actions for education leaders moving forward.

## FOCUSING ON COHERENCE AND COMMON
## UNDERSTANDING, NOT JUST COMMON STANDARDS

The Common Core Learning Standards grow out of a central assumption that
a common focus for instruction can align different parts of the education
system and facilitate coordination, thereby increasing efficiency and performance. The evaluations of the state-level reforms in the 1990s in places like
California and Michigan, however, have already shown that alignment is far
from sufficient to ensure that standards will be implemented effectively or to
see to it that activities across classrooms and schools are coordinated.

Alignment focuses on "lining up" different structures and expectations—
among them standards, curriculum, assessments, and offerings in professional development and preparation programs. But those "aligned" initiatives
may be experienced very differently on the ground, in schools, as they are

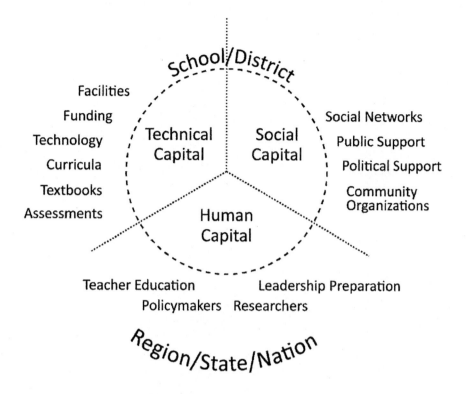

**Figure 10.1. Key Components of Capacity Building**

interpreted and enacted by a host of different people. In order to make initiatives work together, educators need to develop a sense of coherence. Coherence is a state of mind that comes from a common understanding of *how* these different elements fit together (Honig & Hatch, 2004).

In turn, common understanding and coherence grow out of the connections and relationships among people that facilitate the flow of information, resources, and knowledge. Sharing information, knowledge, and resources makes it possible for individuals and groups to coordinate their activities and develop a common sense of what they are supposed to being doing and why they are doing it. Leaders can delegate and distribute responsibilities more effectively, and members of schools and districts can take initiative and act independently in ways that are consistent and reinforcing.

## FOSTERING SOCIAL CONNECTIONS AND COHERENCE
## AT THE SYSTEM LEVEL

The fact that high-performing countries like Singapore and Finland have common learning standards and what appears to be greater alignment in their educational systems often serves as evidence of the need for the Common Core. In these countries, however, common standards and alignment are accompanied by explicit efforts to bring people from different parts of the education system together. These efforts facilitate the development of informal social networks that cross schools and sectors and contribute to common understanding and coherence. In Finland, for example, a nationwide curriculum renewal process has taken place almost every ten years since the 1970s, when the Finnish comprehensive education system was established. The latest renewal launched a new national curriculum framework in 2014, and municipalities will create aligned local curricular frameworks in 2016.

In Finland, in particular, the wide engagement of multiple stakeholders in the renewal effort creates opportunities for many individuals and groups to connect with one another and to reestablish their understanding of the goals of the education system. The last two renewal cycles have engaged key education stakeholders throughout the process. Numerous curriculum groups have been at work developing the guidelines and objectives in each subject and aspect of the core curriculum. Teachers are at the center of these committees, though the committees also include school leaders, municipal administrators, teacher educators, and researchers, among others (and many of those other representatives have themselves been teachers at some point in time). In addition, an advisory board overseeing the whole process includes a cross-section of representatives of teachers, school leaders, parents, students, textbook publishers, researchers, teacher educators, ethnic groups (for instance, representatives of the Sami people), and municipalities.

In past revision cycles, there were opportunities to give feedback on the draft curriculum before it was formally adopted, but the latest revision has been the most open of all. Surveys were sent to all the municipalities so that they can share their responses to initial drafts; municipalities and schools were encouraged to share and discuss the initial proposals with parents and students; and initial drafts of the curriculum were made available online so that anyone who wants to can provide feedback.

Of course, such an open process can be unwieldy, but the wide engagement of teachers, leaders, teacher educators, textbook publishers, researchers, parents, students, and others in the process creates social connections that facilitate the sharing of information and knowledge about the changes *long before those changes are actually made*. In fact, the working committees and feedback process have been going on since 2012, well before the adoption of the new core curriculum was scheduled to be adopted in 2014 and long before the required development of new local curriculum in 2016. This means that those who are involved in supporting the work of teachers and students—like teacher educators and textbook publishers—are already getting a sense of where the revisions are heading and what kinds of changes they will need to make so that the whole system is ready for the implementation of the new local curriculum.

More than a mere adjustment to ensure alignment, the curriculum renewal process serves as an extension of the collective, nation-building effort that Finland launched to create the basic education system in the first place (Sahlberg, 2011). Curriculum renewal in Finland provides an opportunity for those all across the country to recommit themselves to a national enterprise and to develop the common understanding and sense of coherence that can help them to carry it out.

## BUILDING SOCIAL NETWORKS AT THE DISTRICT LEVEL

Unfortunately, the coherence and common focus central to higher-performing education systems may not develop in the United States without more explicit efforts to develop social connections across schools and districts. In fact, several key aspects of conventional schooling and the design and implementation of the Common Core may actually exacerbate the extent of incoherence that many U.S. educators are experiencing. For example:

- The extent of the standards may mean that Common Core–aligned materials end up addressing and emphasizing different aspects of the standards.
- The different approaches, modalities, and technologies associated with different Common Core curricula and assessments may lead educators to see them as conflicting and overwhelming.
- The variety of educators' roles and responsibilities—for teaching and leading different grade levels and subjects, for example—may lead them to view their work on the Common Core as separate and distinct.
- The demands of dealing with many other regulations, policies, and reform initiatives at the same time as the implementation of the Common Core may contribute to an overall sense of fragmentation (Hatch, 2002).

While it is too early to tell how often Common Core implementation may devolve into separate strands of work, a recent study of four districts in New Jersey illustrates the challenges. Those four districts include a mix of small to midsize districts serving a variety of different communities, ranging from low to high performing and from low to high poverty. Yet, surveys that document how often central office administrators, principals, assistant principals, and curriculum supervisors talk to one another about the Common Core show the same basic pattern: relatively limited connections, particularly be-tween building leaders and curriculum supervisors. These results suggest that supervisors and building leaders may not be talking together about the Com-mon Core, increasing the chances that they may be giving the teachers differ-ent messages about the very initiative that is supposed to bring everyone together.

Adding to the complications, the conventional structure of schools separ-ates teachers and administrators into different levels and disciplines (and usually into separate classrooms, departments, meetings, and buildings). As a consequence, despite the emphasis on common standards, Common Core implementation may well end up fragmenting into separate meetings and initiatives in which teachers and administrators interact primarily with col-leagues who work at the same level and in the same departments.

New Jersey's efforts illustrate the difficulty of trying to implement the Common Core in the midst of a number of other major policy initiatives. In New Jersey, work on the Common Core has ramped up at the same time as the development of new policies on teacher evaluation. Like those in other states, these policies have required districts to implement new evaluation procedures that include a substantial increase in the number of times teachers need to be observed. In addition, districts are expected to come up with ratings for teachers that take into account the results of the observations as well as the results from other measures, including test scores. These changes have included the adoption of general observational frameworks that often apply across levels and disciplines.

Correspondingly, in the New Jersey districts surveyed, central office ad-ministrators, building leaders and curriculum supervisors have had more op-portunities to meet together in training and professional development ses-sions focused on the frameworks. Furthermore, in some cases at least, the heavy burden of observing individual teachers multiple times has severely limited the time that all district administrators have to meet to talk about the Common Core and other initiatives. Under these conditions, over a three-year period, the administrators in the four districts studied were more likely to be talking to one another about teacher evaluation than about the Common Core. Furthermore, while supervisors and building leaders were not talking together about teacher evaluation that much, they were doing so more often than they were about the Common Core.

In short, even though the Common Core is designed to be an overarching initiative that helps focus and drive other efforts, work on the Common Core was more likely to be carried out in these districts by separate groups and individuals. Furthermore, work on teacher evaluation was more likely to bring administrators together with a common focus. It is important to recog-nize that it is impossible to know the extent to which the simultaneous implementation of new policies on teacher evaluation and of the Common

Core contributes to improvements in student learning. But the key point is that these examples suggest that the Common Core rollout may not help create a more coordinated and coherent system unless explicit efforts are made to connect individuals and groups across levels, disciplines, and roles.

## NEXT STEPS FOR THE COMMON CORE

The theory and assumptions behind the Common Core suggest that higher shared standards will stimulate a number of developments that could help improve instruction. These include the creation of new curricula, assessments, and other resources, as well as new professional development activities to build knowledge and expertise. But even if these new resources and activities seem aligned, they are not sufficient to drive system-wide improvements. In order to take advantage of the Common Core to ensure that all students reach higher standards of learning, education leaders also need to foster the development of the relationships and social connections that support common understanding and coherence. To do so, education leaders can take several key steps including establishing clear priorities and a common focus, developing connections among individuals and groups who do not always work together, and establishing mechanisms that support regular review and reflection on the priorities and connections that are and are not being made.

## DEVELOP A COMMON FOCUS

To go beyond alignment and begin to create coherence, educators can identify specific emphases and priorities in the Common Core to guide the work on the ground. The key "shifts" in instruction that Common Core architects have articulated reflect one attempt to identify some priorities that may help educators to make sense of the considerable scope of the Common Core. Similarly, school districts can establish instructional expectations that highlight particular standards that respond to identified local needs. Those expectations can provide a common focus for activity, and can clearly spell out how the other initiatives underway in a district can support the priorities in the Common Core.

Establishing these priorities and making these connections, however, depend on deliberate efforts by education leaders to "bridge" and "buffer"—to help the members of their schools, districts, and states see the links between different initiatives and to protect them from the slew of other demands that may distract them from focusing on their priorities (Hatch, 2009). In short, educators can't rely on alignment to drive improvement. They have to drive improvement by making sense of the Common Core and using it to pursue the goals that matter to them, their students, and their community.

## CREATE OPPORTUNITIES FOR CONNECTIONS ACROSS SITES AND ROLES

Regular opportunities for educators in different parts of the school system to connect with one another can foster and sustain common understanding. Initiatives to engage teachers and administrators in looking at the relationship between the standards at different levels and establishing priorities for Common Core implementation may be a particularly powerful vehicle for such connections. These examinations make visible the need for those at different levels to collaborate. Additionally, reviewing and reflecting on students' development over time provides a basis for meaningful joint work in the future.

Explicit and strategic efforts to connect supervisors, site leaders, and central office administrators can also create a powerful triangle of relationships that may help mitigate the tendency for work on instruction to devolve into separate silos. These individuals can serve as "hubs" and "connectors," sharing the responsibility for facilitating the flow of information about the challenges and successes of Common Core implementation across groups that may not normally be connected. Periodic reviews of the communication channels and activities related to the Common Core can also reveal the extent to which different administrators are talking to one another and are (or are not) likely to be on the same page.

## ESTABLISH MECHANISMS FOR REGULAR REVIEW AND RENEWAL

In order to build common understanding and a sense of the priorities that can drive improvement efforts, schools, districts, and even states can create mechanisms that engage many stakeholders in reflecting on the Common Core and their implementation. While the kind of extensive national engagement in curriculum renewal in Finland may seem impossible in the United States, schools, districts, and even states can develop some of the same kinds of periodic review mechanisms to foster a common understanding of the Common Core.

Education leaders can engage many members of their communities in reviewing the standards and identifying key priorities, with the expectation of revisiting those priorities periodically. Even without putting in place a formal review process, school and district leaders can create opportunities for educators, parents, and students to come together and look at the curriculum and assessments used to respond to the Common Core. Looking together at student work in particular can help focus conversations on what shifting to the Common Core means for students. Doing so also provides a foundation for parents and educators to develop a common understanding of what needs to be done to help improve students' learning.

Of course, not all stakeholders need detailed knowledge of standards in every level or discipline, or of all the strategies employed to address the standards. But developing a wider understanding of how common standards can benefit all students, and increasing awareness of what's happening in schools, can help alleviate some of the conflicting demands and expectations that many schools and educators face.

These kinds of initiatives depend on educators who embrace the risks and uncertainty that can come from making their work public, but that willingness makes it harder to reduce teaching and learning to simplistic scores and short-term benchmarks. By creating opportunities for those inside and outside schools to come together, educators can support the broader conversation about what schools are doing and why they are doing it that education in a democracy demands.

In the end, increasing student learning depends on developing powerful tools and resources, related knowledge and skills, and the relationships among people and organizations that can help them integrate their work. Relationships and social connections, in particular, provide access to information, ideas, and expertise that help educators build their skills and knowledge as well as develop networks of allies who share a common understanding of what needs to be done to reach higher standards for all. This is the kind of coherent system that supports the development of the professional and collective agency needed to take advantage of policies and to make improvements in classroom practice on a large scale.

## NOTES

1. The work described in this chapter benefited from the generous support of the Panasonic Foundation and the Fulbright Fellowship Program as well as from discussions and feedback from colleagues in a Panasonic-sponsored network of superintendents.

*Chapter Eleven*

# Intelligently Partnering for Common Core Implementation

## Donald J. Peurach

For many schools, leaders, and teachers, the Common Core State Standards movement has created pressure to act immediately. In some cases, the urgency is shared. Leaders and teachers need to collaborate to improve core educational activities in their schools if they are to demonstrate solid performance on new state assessments and avoid sanctions. In other cases, the urgency is much more personal, with new evaluation schemes linking the professional and personal fortunes of individual leaders and teachers directly to student performance on these assessments.

While some schools and school personnel will be able to respond positively, many others will struggle to imagine, invent, and implement new ways of supporting students in meeting new standards for performance. Moreover, few will have trusted sources to which they can turn, as colleagues in their personal networks are unlikely to be any further down the Common Core road than they are.

That leaves many school and district leaders and teachers with little choice but to turn to new, external sources of support to improve their core educational activities. These sources might include local, regional, and state education agencies; professional associations; publishers; and nonprofit and for-profit program providers. Yet these organizations are experiencing exactly the same pressure for reinvention as schools, leaders, and teachers. And again, while some will be able to respond positively, many others will be struggling to quickly imagine, invent, and implement new ways of assisting schools in responding positively to the new challenges of the Common Core.

And that's the rub. Schools, leaders, and teachers are not working in a *reformed* system immediately able to support schools in improving their core educational capabilities in response to the Common Core. Rather, they are working in a *reforming* system that is itself learning how to do just that.

If that's the rub, then a fundamental challenge faced by schools, leaders, and teachers is that of "intelligently partnering" for Common Core implementation: developing the understandings needed to identify external partners with which to collaborate in learning new ways of improving the core educational capabilities of schools.

This is no simple matter, particularly given the marketing rhetoric and hype that so often fogs efforts to identify and select partners for improvement. Yet it is *the* essential matter. Individuals, organizations, and agencies throughout the educational system must learn to work together in fundamentally new ways on the core educational activities in schools if students are to learn more ambitious academic content and perform at higher standards.

The good news is that some enterprises are actually providing new forms of support to schools and are engaging in new types of collaboration with them. The challenge is actually identifying such organizations, distinguishing them from the many others that are merely packaging the latest untested fads or affixing new labels to outmoded practices.

The purpose of this chapter is to help school personnel act with greater agency and intelligence in forging partnerships that feature new types of collaborative, inter-organizational learning. This intelligence and agency can be exercised at the school level, through the direct selection of partners. They can also be used at the district level, through participation in district-level deliberations about potential partners.

## NEW FORMS OF SUPPORT AND COLLABORATION

For nearly a quarter century, policy initiatives at the state and national level have given rise to "standards-based reform," with schools newly accountable for ensuring that their students perform at high levels on state assessments.

Over this same period, the federal government and large philanthropists have invested heavily in the creation of new types of nongovernmental enterprises to partner with schools to improve their core educational operations. They have also created funding opportunities to support schools in partnering with these enterprises.

What does an ideal partner look like? Although there is no single right answer to this question, effective partners for this era of standards-based reform can be described by the new forms of support they provide to schools, as well as by their collaborative approach.

## SUPPORT

Within the reforming market for school-improvement services, some enterprises provide targeted interventions addressing particular needs in schools, with schools then responsible for integrating targeted interventions into coherent instructional programs. Examples of targeted interventions include new textbooks, assessments, data warehouses, and coaching schemes. Others are much broader in scope, including large-scale "school improvement networks" in which a central hub organization collaborates with schools to enact multi-component, coordinated, school-wide improvement programs.[1] Examples include networks supported by comprehensive school reform providers, charter management organizations, education management organizations, and lead turnaround partners.

No matter how targeted or broad, though, successful enterprises provide much more extensive guidance and support than in the past for improving the core educational activity in schools.[2] Beyond describing new structures and cultures to be recreated in schools, these enterprises provide detailed *designs for practice* that describe exactly who needs to do what, in coordination with others, to support improvements in student performance. For example, a detailed design for practice would include detail about what exactly students and teachers are to do in enacting their roles in instruction; what coaches are to do in providing support to school leaders; and what school leaders are to do in managing and coordinating the program.

Moreover, rather than simply handing schools these designs for practice, these enterprises are matching them with efforts to develop *capabilities for practice* though the use of detailed formal guidance and extensive practice-based professional development. To provide such extensive support, the hub organizations in these enterprises are developing new capabilities for design, coaching, and research and evaluation uncommon among local and state education agencies. For example, some hub organizations have entire teams of program developers collaborating to create material and digital resources for use by students and teachers; large networks of coaches and trainers who can support the effective use of those resources; and teams of evaluators that observe, measure, and analyze classroom activities and student performance.

## COLLABORATION

While sometimes assumed to function as cookie-cutter enterprises in which schools implement "off-the-shelf" improvement programs, at least some of these networks play against type. Specifically, some operate as *learning systems*. These are enterprises in which hub organizations and schools collaborate to produce, use, and refine the practical knowledge needed both to navigate turbulence and uncertainty in environments and to improve student performance at scale.[3]

In several large-scale networks that have been recognized for improving practice and student outcomes in large numbers of schools, these learning processes depend heavily on the careful coordination of two strategies for implementation that have long been viewed as being at cross purposes: *fidelity of implementation* and *school-based adaptation*. By skillfully managing the coordination of these two approaches, these enterprises have managed to harness the positive aspects of both of these strategies while avoiding many of their pitfalls. Here's how they do it.

During initial implementation, the strategies focus on faithfully implementing hub-provided guidance. One goal of faithful implementation is to establish base-level knowledge, capabilities, and performance and, with that, to begin to create a new sense of possibility and responsibility. Another goal is to stem a rapid regression to past practice. A third goal of faithful implementation is to create an infrastructure for professional practice and learning that is uncommon among historically fragmented schools. This infrastructure would include common instructional values, methods, language, artifacts, assessments, and experiences—all emerging from shared, mutually dependent work.

After the strategies are in place, schools can leverage this infrastructure as the basis for collaborative reflection and learning among teachers and leaders, thus creating potential to adapt hub-provided guidance that is responsive to local needs. Operating at the center, the hub monitors activity both within the network and among other research, development, and reform communities; incorporates favorable adaptations and additions to the program; and feeds improvements through the network via formal guidance and professional learning opportunities.

With such a support-based, collaborative approach, schools do not function as downstream recipients of a centrally diffused model, nor do they use high-level principles and guidelines as a basis for incubating their own, school-specific solutions. Rather, schools function as active collaborators in a widely distributed, knowledge-producing enterprise.

## VETTING POTENTIAL PARTNERS FOR IMPROVEMENT

It would be a mistake to confuse the forward progress described above with a new normal. While a small number of networks exemplify these characteristics, many others fall short. Thus, in reaching out to agencies and organizations to support Common Core implementation, the challenge for schools, leaders, and teachers is to discern between networks that exemplify these characteristics and those that do not.

A strong first step is using data thoughtfully and responsibly, both to identify strengths and needs within the school, and to begin searching for potential partners. Rather than succumbing to the usual faddism associated with educational reforms, doing so should include reviewing such resources as the What Works Clearinghouse and the Best Evidence Encyclopedia to identify effective programs with potential to address local needs. Yet these resources are themselves emerging, with only a small number of programs having undergone the type of rigorous evaluations that they require.

Given the uncertainty about what does and does not work, a strong second step is to evaluate potential partners as learning systems in which hubs and schools collaborate to produce, use, and refine the knowledge and capabilities needed to respond positively to the press to improve student performance. Schools can take this next step by following the developmental evaluation process described below.[4]

## GATHERING EVIDENCE

The process begins with generating a wide and deep pool of information about the design and operations of the enterprises under consideration. Examples of useful resources include promotional and sales materials; program materials for use by teachers and school leaders; and training materials for use by external coaches. These materials, in turn, should be complemented by conversations with program developers, trainers, and leaders, as well as conversations with other schools, leaders, and teachers participating in the enterprise.

The ease with which you can track down this information, and how open the enterprise is to answering your questions, would be positive, early indicators of transparency and collaboration. Difficulty on either of these fronts would be an early red flag.

## ANALYZING THE EVIDENCE

The process continues with analyzing this information by filtering it through five questions. Each of these questions provides a particular perspective on the enterprise as a learning system.

- *Does the enterprise have a history of continuous learning and improvement, and a strategy for achieving it?* Begin by looking for statements about collaboration between the hub and the school concerning commitments to continuous learning and improvement. But as the saying goes, talk is cheap. Evidence of actual improvement based on a strategy of continuous learning might include multiple editions and versions of key material and digital resources.

- *Does the enterprise have a clearly explained and well-thought-out design for practice?* Beyond describing structures and culture, such a design would provide details about *exactly who* is supposed to do *exactly what*. It would include formal descriptions of essential roles, the qualifications for those roles, principles detailing responsibilities and coordination among roles, and standards and rubrics for assessing the enactment of those roles.
- *Does the enterprise provide guidance and support for re-creating capabilities for base-level practices in schools?* This would be demonstrated by a strong, literal message of "fidelity of implementation" running throughout guidance and training, along with detailed guidance and training to explain and model the faithful enactment of specific, practical tasks associated with particular roles.
- *Does the enterprise provide guidance and support for re-creating capabilities for adaptive, locally responsive use?* Look for strong messages of school-level ownership of the change process, along with guidance and support for school-based analysis, evaluation, problem solving, decision making, design, and other discretionary activity.
- *Does the hub organization have the infrastructure and capabilities to support continuous, enterprise-wide learning and improvement?* Look for a communication infrastructure for exchanging knowledge and information among hubs and schools. Other evidence might include opportunities, resources, and capabilities for analyzing school performance and outcomes (for example, via formal methods of design-based implementation research) and for rapid prototyping and small-scale evaluation.

## INTERPRETING THE EVIDENCE

The next step is to interpret answers to the five questions to discern ways the enterprise does and does not operate as a learning system. One way of doing this is to identify a given enterprise as one of four primary types: a shell enterprise, a diffusion enterprise, an incubation enterprise, and an evolutionary enterprise.

A *shell enterprise* is the American default: an organization that places a primary emphasis on schools adopting common structures and cultures, with little or no emphasis on developing the knowledge and capabilities to work within new structures and culture to devise, enact, and adapt new practices. In a shell enterprise, schools are left largely to go it alone.

A *diffusion enterprise* is one that attends closely to practice, though primarily through fidelity of implementation: that is, faithful enactment of proven practices in new schools. A diffusion enterprise often lacks supports for (and even discourages) school-based adaptation. It also often lacks mechanisms for "feeding back" and circulating new knowledge as it emerges throughout the enterprise, as there is little emphasis on supporting schools in generating new knowledge. While a diffusion enterprise can support quickly establishing new, base-level operations, the schools themselves are left to develop their own capabilities for continuous learning and improvement.

An *incubation enterprise* is also one that attends closely to practice, though primarily through local adaptation—that is, by guiding and supporting schools in operationalizing principles of practice in locally responsive ways. An incubation enterprise often lacks supports for the faithful enactment of established methods and procedures and even discourages such practices. It also often lacks mechanisms for "feeding back" and circulating new knowledge as it emerges throughout the enterprise because such knowledge is often viewed as school specific. While an incubation enterprise can support schools in charting a new way forward, it also challenges them to develop and successfully enact new base-level operations that deviate from established practices. Further, the school-specific nature of solutions complicates collaborative problem solving among the hub and schools.

An *evolutionary enterprise* is one that most resembles the type of idealized "learning system" described earlier, with hubs and schools collaborating to produce, use, and refine practical knowledge. An evolutionary enterprise has strengths along all five of the dimensions that are the focus of the five analytical questions: strategies for learning and improvement that emphasize hub/school collaboration; detailed designs for practice; extensive support for base-level practice; extensive support for adaptive use; and well-developed learning infrastructure in the hub organization.

## ADDITIONAL CONVERSATION

While an evolutionary enterprise may be the ideal, such enterprises are also likely to be rare. After all, the leaders of these enterprises are in the same boat as schools, as they are also learning to work in new ways in response to reforming, and uncertain, environments.

As such, the process concludes with using all of the evidence and analysis described above as a foundation for additional conversation with potential partners. In these conversations, schools, leaders, and teachers will be empowered to ask probing questions about how the enterprise is succeeding and struggling in guiding and supporting schools. They will also be able to discern whether or not the enterprise is poised to *evolve to evolve*: that is, to advance beyond operating as a shell, diffusion, or incubation enterprise toward a fuller, evolutionary approach to learning and collaborating with schools.

## CLOSING THOUGHTS

As schools position themselves to respond to the pressures of the Common Core, they will no doubt encounter an abundance of agencies and organizations touting their programs and services as "Common Core aligned." Yet such marketing rhetoric says little about the capabilities of these agencies and organizations to support schools in effecting deep change in structures, culture, and practice.

The aim of this chapter has been to help schools, leaders, and teachers move beyond marketing rhetoric by developing understandings needed to intelligently partner with agencies and organizations that support the improvement of the core educational activities in schools. This includes potential partners that have already developed replicable and effective programs. It also includes potential partners that are collaborating with schools to "learn their way through" the uncertainty and complexity of the Common Core.

To be sure, this business of intelligently partnering is likely to be complicated in practice. Some schools will have the resources and latitude to work on their own behalf. Others will need to collaborate (and to assert their interests) in the district-level decision-making process. Still others, unfortunately, will be boxed out of such decision-making processes.

Further, other issues are sure to come into play. These could include managing concerns about the top-down, outside/inside nature of these partnerships or addressing the complexities of for-profit vendors supporting the improvement of public schools. Other challenges might involve building a strong coalition of teachers, leaders, parents, and other constituents in electing partners with which to ultimately work.

Finally, selecting partners involves considerations beyond their effectiveness and learning potential that must be brought to bear, including the extent to which teachers and leaders connect on a personal level with program coaches and trainers, and including the longevity and stability of the broader enterprise.

That said, the preceding positions schools, leaders, and teachers to leverage available resources with greater intelligence and agency in responding to the collective and personal pressure to improve their core educational activities. And that, after all, is the central challenge of Common Core implementation.

## NOTES

1. See Peurach & Glazer (2012) and Glazer & Peurach (2013) for a discussion of school improvement networks as a strategy for large-scale educational reform in the United States.
2. See Peurach (2011), Cohen et al. (2014), and Rowan et al. (2009) for detailed accounts of more extensive support as provided in comprehensive school reform programs.
3. For detailed accounts of these learning dynamics, see Peurach & Glazer (2012).

4. See Peurach, Glazer & Lenhoff (2014) for a detailed exposition of the framework for developmental evaluation.

*Chapter Twelve*

# Contracting for Digital Education in the Common Core Era

## Patricia Burch, Andrew L. LaFave, and Annalee Good

Purchasing digital tools to support instruction is a process fraught with confusion and uncertainty. Administrators and teachers facing such decisions often find themselves squeezed between two pressure points with no easy way forward. On the one hand, they face pressure to acquire digital products or be seen as falling behind relative to other schools. On the other hand, they face pressure to use the tools they have already acquired in the most effective way.

The smattering of research on digital educational technology that has turned up to date is largely mixed: What works in one school for one group of students may be ineffective in other schools with different groups of kids. These kinds of inconclusive results even manifest themselves as differences between classrooms in the same building—a situation familiar to anyone who has spent any time working in a school. What this means for practitioners is that it pays to be skeptical of vendor claims that a product has been universally "proven." The research a firm is drawing on might be perfectly sound for the specific context in which it was studied, but the product that boosted achievement rates by 30 percent in Des Moines might be a waste of money in Detroit.

Wide disparities in school funding are equally troubling when it comes to digital tools. A wealthy district in the suburbs can afford to sift through five or six programs to find one that works for it, while a poor district in the city can only afford to buy a single product and hope that it is more wheat than chaff. Rather than reducing the achievement gap between various demographic groups—a claim that vendors often implicitly make—the difference in per-pupil funding between districts means that these products can actually make the achievement gap worse.

Wealthier districts can afford exciting synchronous curriculum, where students conduct science experiments online, with assistance from expert scientists at local universities as part of the districts' college-ready programs. Whereas schools in under-resourced communities may have to choose between quality curriculum and a working computer on which to run the curriculum. The wealthier school districts already have the hardware, supported in part by parent donations. In this regard, as the curriculum moves online, economic privilege can breed technological privilege and unequal opportunities to learn.

While acknowledging the way forward is fraught with these and many other challenges, this chapter provides questions to guide educators in their digital technology purchasing decisions, helping them to steer clear of the most dangerous and costly obstacles.

## TWO QUESTIONS FOR EDUCATORS TO ASK WHEN PURCHASING DIGITAL TECHNOLOGY

Educators must ask themselves and potential vendors two critical questions when considering the use of digital tools to help achieve Common Core standards:

- **Are the tools or services being offered actually aligned with the CCSS or other standards for which you will be held accountable?** Most, if not all, of the products provided by education services firms are advertised as being "aligned with the Common Core." But the idea of "alignment" can mean many things to many people. Does the definition provided by the vendor line up with your school's or district's definition?
- **Are the tools and services actually going to meet the specific needs of your students?** Many will, but others will not. Understanding exactly what the service or product is intended to address will go a long way toward helping you make an effective choice.

Vendors, through their sales reps and marketing materials, often make claims that appear to address these questions. But it is important for administrators and teachers to recognize—and then continually remind themselves as they wade through vendor marketing materials—that there are no empirically derived "best practices" for answering them. Specifically, there is currently not enough reliable data in two important areas.

First, and perhaps most pressing, is the need for best practices for integrating technology into classroom instruction. Without this knowledge, digital technology implementation in schools will remain stuck in the world of LCD-projector-as-the-new-overhead.

Second is the need to determine how accessible digital technology is across different contexts. In other words, is it at a price point that may make it prohibitive for economically pressed school districts? Is it accessible in terms of users' language preferences? For example, if students are English Language Learners, how adaptive is the tool to their needs? And is it accessible in terms of students' learning differences—can it accommodate the needs of students with disabilities, for example?

Despite the fact that there is little in the way of definitive, research-backed answers to such questions, many vendors' marketing materials often seem to say otherwise. Here, for example, are some representative claims from one vendor's marketing materials, with emphasis added to highlight its claim:

> With [our] new interface, educators can instantly create instructional remediation and enrichment plans based on each student's assessment results, ensuring **that the right instructional support is assigned at the right time for every student**.

Implied here is that some types of support are inherently right, and that these "right" supports will work equally well for every student. These claims are almost certainly backed up by sound research that might come from nationally representative data samples, but it does not guarantee that the interventions will work at all times in all places with all students.

The same vendor also makes claims about connections between its products and personalized instruction, or meeting each student's individual needs wherever they are:

> The [assessment package], available for Grades 3–8, helps educators measure student growth and achievement in this new era of more rigorous standards. Providing educators unique and valuable standards-based reports, [the package] makes it easy to enrich classroom instruction, personalize learning, and **track students' readiness for college and a career**.

Again, the implication is that this product will ensure that *all* students in the client districts will have access to high-quality instruction, instruction that is tailored to their needs rather than batch processed, and that will provide teachers and administrators with a tool to gauge college readiness, a catchphrase in the CCSS. While the potential might exist, in 2015 these claims are still just that: *claims*. In short, the rhetoric outpaces the research. This is not a new problem, but it can be an expensive one for districts.

Understanding the limitations of the research base establishing best practices for the use of digital support tools and services is essential for developing a purchasing plan for a classroom or school. And while the limitations discussed here concern specific claims of effectiveness, this level of scrutiny can also be applied to other vendor claims as well.

Perhaps the most essential marketing claim to investigate is that of "standards alignment." This claim often takes for granted that "we" all "know" what it means for a product to be "standards aligned." But do we? This advertising copy, from a different vendor, represents the kinds of glossing over that educators often encounter (emphasis added):

> Many of [our] award-winning products align with the new Common Core State Standards (CCSS) in Mathematics and English Language Arts and the Next Generation Science Standards (NGSS). On this page, you'll find free, easy-to-use guides that pinpoint **exactly which standards line up with the products you own and those you're considering purchasing.**

Nowhere is there a definition of what "line up" means, and vendors like this one leave the final understanding of what "alignment" means to their clients. Merely listing the standards that connect to a particular curriculum isn't proof of standards alignment. (It is important to acknowledge that, in this case, the tools being offered are free. But the actual curriculum materials that those tools describe are not free.)

By contrast, consider this example from a different vendor. This copy comes from a description of a series of reports that the vendor makes available to current and prospective clients (emphasis added):

> [Our firm] provides alignment reports to customers to show how the skills within each product align to the skills within academic standards. The alignment report **presents all of the academic standards for a specific state/ agency with the aligned . . . product skills indented below each standard.**

By making this kind of information available to educators, firms can create an environment that supports instruction and makes it easier for administrators and teachers to make informed decisions for their schools. Rather than making an elegant claim about the degree of alignment between their products and the standards, this vendor has created a quick and easy tool to facilitate a purchasing decision. Here, it is not that the product is aligned, but rather that each product addresses a set of skills that may or may not fit within the framework of the CCSS. The vendor leaves the final determination up to the client.

The final example comes from an entirely different kind of vendor. While the other three are for-profit firms, this vendor is a not-for-profit organization that offers its tools to educators for free. Instead of making claims about alignment and implying that clients should trust the firm, this vendor makes alignment-evaluation tools available to clients, encouraging them to draw their own conclusions (emphasis added):

> [Our standards-aligned products] can be validated using a "jurying" process that confirms the modules' alignment to Common Core demands. Jurying also looks at how richly the tasks and modules engage academic content to build CCSS-aligned skills. **Jurying can provide thoughts on how to improve each module, and it is also used to identify modules that are ready to share and to spotlight those that reach the especially high standards of "exemplary" ... design [from our organization].**

All the vendors whose marketing materials are quoted in this chapter have the same goal: to improve student learning. The difference is that some vendors are less transparent about the strategies they use to secure that improvement. Not all vendors talk about their products in the same way. Informed consumers need to ask themselves and their prospective vendors a series of probing questions to make sure that the needs of the vendor and the needs of the students come together in a way that is acceptable.

## FOUR QUESTIONS FOR SCHOOL-BASED EMPOWERMENT

One positive corollary to the adoption of the CCSS has been a move—albeit a slower one—to devolve centralized decision-making power to local control. This change has vested local school boards and school principals with the unprecedented power to make key instructional decisions that will impact the communities that matter most to schools. With this greater empowerment, however, has come an increased sense of responsibility; in many cases, the central office can no longer be blamed for missteps.

In this environment, it has become even more essential for school-based decision makers to make the right choices for their students. Again, in order to make the right choices, educators must know (a) whether the digital products and services actually aligned to the CCSS; and (b) whether these services actually serve the specific needs of students. Finding accurate answers to these two important questions is made even harder given the blind spots in the research and the kinds of claims vendors often make. In the absence of clear, robust, and research-based information directing educators to the correct answers, potential consumers of education services should ask—both of themselves and of their vendors—a set of four sub-questions. Finding answers to these questions will go a long way toward ensuring that administrators and teachers get the services and tools actually aligned to the CCSS and their students' needs, and ultimately avoid programs that waste scarce school resources.

## What Drives the Digital Curriculum?

The first question has to do with the forces that have shaped the digital curriculum market. One way of thinking about this question is in terms of whether the curriculum is designed and managed by a centralized vendor who leases the curriculum to schools as opposed to curriculum that is designed for local adaptation and teacher input. Another aspect of this question is assessing the intent and know-how of the company behind the curriculum.

When schools approach or are approached by a vendor, the first level of due diligence should involve understanding where the vendor came from, who runs the firm, and how it has come to be a developer of the types of tools or services under consideration. If the answer to these questions ends up being something like "they're just the biggest vendor around so we should trust them," consider going deeper. Large firms are often excellent at what they do, but is market share the best reason to contract with them? Maybe, maybe not. Interrogating both the vendor's place in the market and a school's own needs are an important place to start.

## What Drives Digital Instruction?

The second question turns the focus from curriculum to instruction, considering the forces that have shaped the digital instruction market. The instructional setting and the role of the teacher are moving, appropriately, to the forefront of CCSS policy debates. At the core of the debates are questions about the role of the teacher and the distribution of instructional resources. On one end of the continuum is the expectation reflected in the design of both hardware and software that a live teacher still has primary responsibility for students' learning. In contrast, the implicit understanding on the other end of the continuum is that a digital environment can function without a teacher and should be primarily software driven.

Another way to approach this question is asking not whether, but if and under what circumstances, to use technology as part of instructional strategy. Granted, technology exists; standards and common sense tell us that we must integrate it into our schools. But for a specific product, why is it important to use digital tools to teach in the way supported by that product? Many digital tools provide meaningful benefits to schools and students, but others are solutions in search of a problem. Taking a digital approach to teaching computer programming languages makes sense; moving music performance classes to an asynchronous online platform does not.

Some teachers are nervous about the move toward digital instruction. Others are ecstatic. Most are likely somewhere in between. Where there is common ground is that digital instruction, if it continues at this pace, will change what it means to be a teacher. The design of some tools seems to assume that the curriculum will do most of the teaching. The curriculum replaces the teacher. The only live interaction the student has is with a 1-800 number for troubleshooting technology issues. On the other end of the continuum is digital instruction that places a live teacher either in the classroom or in a virtual classroom on the student's computer screen. The student can get help from the teacher by raising her hand, or a virtual hand, as it were, and get answers in real time.

The CCSS are premised on the principle that it is not enough to have good curriculum—in other words, that teachers matter. This is backed by solid research. If software alone is driving CCSS instruction, students are very likely to be shortchanged.

## What Drives Assessment and Access to Data?

Many of the policy conversations are focused on how we can nail down accurate data, explain or define the accuracy of the data, or compel educators to use the data. Beneath these questions is a larger issue that has to do with control. Who dictates what counts as data? And who controls the data itself?

The easiest answers here are that standards drive assessment, and the need to improve achievement on those assessments demands access to testing data. Both of these answers are true, but when purchasing an assessment product from a vendor that centrally controls your school's data, it pays to ask whether or not the services on offer will meet your school's identified need.

Will the assessment data of the school's students be fully accessible to the school, or will it be centrally warehoused by the vendor and only available to schools in aggregate form?

Can the data be used by the vendor for other purposes, or does it remain the property of the school? What happens to the data if the district decides to change vendors down the line?

In other words, is the product actually about measuring student achievement, or is it mostly about mining student data for the secondary market?

How can districts and vendors work together to be sure that commercial or political interests don't trump the interests of students?

This is the most difficult question to ask and answer. Ideally, schools and districts would be involved in the development of the services or tools they plan to consume, and for some large districts, this may be the case. But while it is easy for districts like the Los Angeles Unified School District or the Chicago Public Schools to command access to a vendor's development process, it is much more difficult for small, poor, or rural districts to extract the same kinds of concessions. Why would a vendor collaborate with a district that only represents a few thousand dollars' worth of purchasing power when they can spend their time servicing the billion-dollar contract being offered by New York City?

For districts that are unable to be part of the development process themselves, the question becomes one of recognition. Does the vendor under consideration make it clear who developed the product? Does that list of developers include educators, and, if so, are they well-known professionals who are respected in the field? If educators were not involved, is it easy to understand why not?

## CONCLUSION

Getting answers to the two central questions suggested earlier in this chapter, or at least starting the dialogue about them, is at least as important as how school and district administrators interact and negotiate with vendors' representatives. This has always been the case, but is particularly true now, as companies move to aggressively market digital instructional services and products that are advertised as helping practitioners successfully implement CCSS.

Reframing the conversation around CCSS means thinking seriously about holding vendors accountable in all aspects of the contracting process for the underlying principles of CCSS, high-quality and equitable opportunities to learn, and continuous improvement. In the absence of sustained scrutiny, we lose the potential of digital education to push a broader agenda for more equitable distribution of resources in public education. This would be an enormous loss.

*Part 4 Introduction*

# Navigating Politics in the Common Core Era

## Jonathan A. Supovitz

In the traditional view, politics precedes policy. The classical notion is that the political arena is where policy ideas get incubated, debated, and perforated. If an idea can successfully navigate this gauntlet to become an enacted policy, then the political din recedes to clamor from the fringes and the focus becomes implementation. But it just ain't so anymore, if it ever really was. Now we are in a perpetual political epoch where the political debate continues to swirl around districts and schools unabated, even as educators must implement state law. In such a context, how do practitioners navigate the politics of the Common Core, even as they engage with implementation challenges? What is the relationship between politics and implementation anyways? And what do educators need to know about the political debates about the standards? These questions are the focus of this section of the book.

In chapter 13, Pennsylvania State University educational historian David Gamson chases academic expectations back through American history and shows how their tail stretches back to the Puritans, who took expectations very seriously. Gamson then repels us back through different iterations of standards to the present. In doing so, he provides us with important perspectives on ongoing efforts to specify what children should know and are able to do and gives us useful contrasts against which to both compare our current efforts and to avoid previously trodden pitfalls.

Patrick McGuinn, a political scientist at Drew University in New Jersey, takes us in chapter 14 on a tour of the political opposition to the CCSS so we can understand both the diverse constituencies that have come together in opposition to the standards as well as the arguments that underlie their positions. McGuinn points out that many of the disagreements stem from issues unrelated to educational standards. In doing so, McGuinn argues that many of the arguments against standards are really proxies for other debates around educational priorities and values.

Political scientists have particular perspectives on policy implementation that can be helpful to practitioners who are trying to navigate standards implementation challenges. In chapter 15, Kathryn McDermott of the University of Massachusetts–Amherst offers ideas for understanding and maintaining perspective while standing in the thick of the implementation challenge. McDermott makes a particularly useful distinction between what she calls "big-P" and "small-p" politics, and argues that the terrain of the small-p is where implementation differences are contested. By walking us through the politics of several recent state and local testing and assessment implementation examples, McDermott shows how important framing considerations can prune or thicket the implementation pathways.

In chapter 16, Jennifer O'Day of the American Institutes for Research provides a case study of California's progress in implementing the CCSS. O'Day, one of the important contributors to the conceptualization of systemic reform in the 1990s, tells the story of how a window of opportunity has opened up in California to achieve deeper standards implementation. By providing a perspective on the political, fiscal, and policy landscapes, she points out lessons for other states and districts. She argues that a long-term systemic approach that combines policy supports and stakeholder relationship building is required to develop both the resources and space to do the challenging and sustained work of instructional improvement in schools and classrooms.

Here are several questions for you and your colleagues to discuss about navigating politics in the Common Core era:

1. How are the national political debates (the big-P politics) about the CCSS and associated policies (testing, curriculum, accountability, etc.) affecting your efforts to implement the CCSS?
2. What are the (small-p) politics of the CCSS like in your local community? Map the sources of support and/or opposition. What kinds of pressure or assistance do these groups exert on you and your organization?
3. What are the (small-p) politics of the CCSS in your school and/or district? What do you see as your role in navigating these politics to influence standards implementation?

*Chapter Thirteen*

# Differences in Common

*A Brief History of American Educational Standards*

David A. Gamson

Since the children of the first colonists cracked open the covers of their *New England Primers* in the crisp autumn air of seventeenth-century Massachusetts, Americans have been worried about educational standards for their pupils. Whether these concerns have been articulated as religious strictures, academic benchmarks, or beliefs about proper deportment and behavior, specifications about student proficiency have both united and divided the nation. Today we call these expectations "standards," and the most recent effort at defining such academic criteria is the Common Core State Standards (CCSS).

The usual approach to explaining the origins of current standards-based reform is to begin with a series of events in the 1980s, such as the 1983 *A Nation at Risk* or an important 1989 educational summit convened by President George H. W. Bush and the nation's governors; and, indeed, these developments marked an important shift in reform strategy. Yet they are not truly the birthplace of standards in our national educational experience.

Although today's Common Core unquestionably has some unique features, practitioners might be surprised to learn that when viewed with a broader historical lens, the CCSS are less a dramatic innovation than the latest iteration of a long legacy of efforts to define academic expectations. This chapter offers a brief history of how educational leaders in the United States have attempted to create academic standards over the past two centuries—focusing especially on successive efforts to create common, uniform academic expectations—and it illustrates how generations of educators have sought to specify and strengthen what students were meant to know and be able to do.

This history is meant to provide a foundation for a better understanding of the use of standards in American society. More attention is given to earlier periods in the nation's history, in part because readers may not be as familiar with those eras, but also because shining a light on these prior developments illuminates just how deeply runs the tendency in our culture to define, discuss, and debate the kinds of knowledge Americans want their children to have.

Why is it useful to review the history of standards? Will such an account help us avoid the repetition of past mistakes, or are we condemned to repeat history? A more useful way to approach this overview might be to invoke the wisdom of Mark Twain. "History doesn't repeat itself," Twain once said, "but it rhymes." The goal of this chapter, then, is less to catalogue a series of academic content changes than it is to attune readers' ears to various rhyming patterns within the history of American education.

## THE AMERICAN COLONIES AND THE NEW REPUBLIC, 1630–1820s

Although many policymakers today believe in high-stakes tests, they had nothing on the Puritans. These early immigrants to the New World faced a series of ominous challenges—not the least of which were illness and starvation—as they established settlements, but the fact that they created schools, enacted education laws, and founded Harvard University, all within the first two decades of their arrival, is a testament to their belief in the importance of education. Indeed, their main schoolbook, *The New England Primer*, essentially served as an early common curriculum for many colonial schoolchildren.

Historians are quick to point out that the incipient educational practices established by the Puritans should not be seen as forerunners of the American school systems; after all, Puritan society was a theocracy wherein the Church and the family held much more gravitas than any school. Moreover, literacy had one central purpose: learning to read the Bible—only then could Puritans gain direct access to the word of God. These beliefs yielded clear expectations: the end goal of education was salvation, the ultimate high-stakes assessment.

Even after the colonies diversified and dispersed, the emphasis on the spread of literacy skills was perhaps the most important factor in unifying the colonies during the eighteenth century. After the Revolutionary War, education continued to preoccupy many of the founding fathers, for they understood the delicate nature of their new republic, and they feared their experiment in democracy could easily falter.

Many of our early national leaders argued that a thoroughly American curriculum would help unify the language and culture of the new nation and insulate its fledging citizens from the flaws of an older and "corrupt" Europe. "The national character is not yet formed," wrote Noah Webster in 1790. Common schools, Webster asserted, would instill in American children "an inviolable attachment to their own country" (quoted in Kaestle, 1983: 6–7).

Early American educational theorists believed in issuing new textbooks that celebrated the heroes of the Revolution and hailed their great deeds. Still, finding agreement on precisely which accomplishments and national heroes to highlight often yielded spirited disagreements. Indeed, John Adams once complained about the "the superstitious veneration that is sometimes paid to General Washington" (quoted in Nash, Crabtree & Dunn, 2000, p. 18). And some early American history textbooks essentially snubbed Thomas Jefferson by devoting more space and attention to Alexander Hamilton.

Although state leaders proposed bills for publicly supported, free schools in the late 1700s and early 1800s, these plans gained little traction. Reformers were more successful in using schoolbooks as a mechanism for diffusion of patriotic views, American linguistic principles, and common cultural ideals. Webster's famous spelling book, for instance, was essential in establishing the rudiments of "American English." Toward the middle of the nineteenth century, market forces sometimes did what reformers could not; the *McGuffey's Readers* and other popular texts often created a de facto uniformity across far-flung schools.

Well into the nineteenth century, we should remember, education was rather rudimentary. Most communities were satisfied if their children gained some fundamental skills in literacy and numeracy. Aside from children of the wealthy, few students continued beyond a few years of schooling.

## COMMON SCHOOLS, 1820s–1880s

As scholars like to point out, the United States has the most decentralized educational system in the world. The reasons for this date back to the origins of local educational institutions established across the nation throughout the mid-nineteenth century. Although there was little statewide support for anything like a system of education in the early 1800s, we should not take this to mean that parents were uninterested in educating their children.

Neighboring groups of parents collaborated to build a local school and hire a teacher. Historians estimate that there may once have been upwards of two hundred thousand school districts (vs. fourteen thousand today), and many of these districts contained merely one school. Such an array of districts scattered across city and countryside offered little guarantee there would be much academic consistency from location to location.

By the 1820s and 1830s, modernizers in the New England and mid-Atlantic states had pushed their legislatures to create state boards, state offices of education, and the legal framework allowing for the establishment of districts. In 1837 Horace Mann, perhaps the most famous nineteenth-century reformer, was appointed as the secretary of education to the newly created State Board of Education in Massachusetts. As he toured schools across his state, Mann quickly became appalled by the erratic instructional practices he witnessed and the wretched conditions of the schoolhouses he visited.

Mid-nineteenth-century Common School reformers like Mann stressed the need for enhanced professionalization, best achieved, they contended, through standardized pedagogical practices and teacher training programs (Mann helped found the first teachers college, or "normal school," in 1839). Greater uniformity in curricula and student textbooks, Common School leaders argued, would also ensure at least a minimum amount of educational opportunity for all public school students. Common School reformers—who described their movement as a crusade—believed emphasis on professional standards would pressure local districts to abandon outmoded practices, to boost the quality of their educational materials, and to raise the expectations they held for their teachers.

Textbooks often stood in as a proxy for a more explicit and thorough curriculum, but Mann understood they could also serve as a device more expedient than system-wide change. "There is a public evil of great magnitude in the multiplicity and diversity of textbooks. They crowd the market and infest the schools," warned Mann in 1838. "One would suppose that there might be uniformity in rudiments, at least;" he complained, "yet the greatest variety prevails. . . . By a change of books, a child is often obliged to unlearn what he had laboriously acquired before" (Massachusetts Annual Report, 1838: 32 [hereafter MA Report]).

It would be a mistake, however, to see Mann as solely concerned about textbooks. In fact, he was apprehensive about overreliance on them, preferring to trust instead in highly knowledgeable teachers. "Teachers should be able to teach subjects," he once said, "not manuals merely" (MA Report, 1841: 48). Moreover, in his appeals to the public, we see his abiding concern about providing something like equal opportunities for the state's children.

To Mann, equalization meant that all children, no matter their station or location, should receive an education that was, if not of high quality, at least reasonably competent. Requiring common textbooks was one way to ensure that poor families, "to whom the expense of school books is sometimes a serious burden," would not have to buy new textbooks if they moved from one district to another (MA Report, 1841: 63). In Mann's view, education served as "the great equalizer of the conditions of men—the balance wheel of the social machinery."

Mann's contemporary, Henry Barnard, the commissioner of education in neighboring Rhode Island (and later the first U.S. commissioner of education), expressed similar worries. "On no one point is there more earnest and general complaint . . . than that of the multiplicity of school books," Barnard wrote in 1845, and he called for "prompt and efficient action on the part of the Legislature" (Barnard, 1846: 17). Solutions would never be reached, Barnard felt, awaiting the independent action of town school boards; legislative action and centralized authority were more effective. Although state superintendents rarely had much real power, they often used a wide variety of tools at their disposal for establishing statewide expectations, including bulletins, annual reports, state-sponsored journals, and teacher institutes.

Proclamations and opinions issued from state capitals often elicited the suspicion of locals, who expressed anxiety about intrusion from higher authorities. For example, a school principal from Watertown, New York, speaking to a 1873 gathering of teachers, acknowledged the need for state authority in schooling but quickly tempered that notion by clarifying: "I do not mean that there should be such centralization of power in the State Board as to produce dead uniformity throughout the state but enough to induce conformity to the curriculum prescribed by the State" (Smith, 1873: 26).

Educational liberty was a treasured characteristic of nineteenth-century schooling, and local leaders bristled when they felt their independence threatened. In 1896, one Georgia district superintendent opposed a proposed state plan to mandate uniformity of textbooks, because it "strikes at the very taproot of good government; because it is undemocratic and despotic; because it would foster a monopoly, beget paternalism and encourage centralization" (Pound, 1897: 112).

Increasing centralization of authority, first locally, then at the state level, was one of the characteristic shifts of nineteenth-century schooling. The tension regarding centralization and decentralization in governance was a distinctive dynamic of industrializing nations of the era. In his *Considerations on Representative Government*, John Stuart Mill concluded that "power may be localized, but knowledge, to be most useful, must be centralized" (Mill, 1861: 290).

By the 1880s and the 1890s, many states had introduced some kind of common standards, whether through required textbooks, certification requirements for teachers, or legislatively mandated coursework. Some state legislatures passed laws requiring the state to provide textbooks for children free of charge; other states even began to print their own textbooks.

The "Course of Study" became one of the most important mechanisms for setting and disseminating baseline academic expectations. Courses of Study, mostly forgotten today, were publications issued by states, counties, and districts throughout the late nineteenth and early twentieth centuries. Part content standards, part curricular guidelines, part lists of recommended textbooks, part pacing guide, part lesson plans, and even part assessment questions, the general purpose of the Course of Study was to outline the minimum quantity of work expected for each grade. They offer clear evidence that educational leaders of the era were highly attentive to setting standards. Though not a direct ancestor of today's standards-based reform, the Courses of Study set a precedent for state authority in educational matters; they also illustrated an early effort by educators to distinguish between standards and curriculum, concepts that were often conflated throughout the century that followed.

Kansas's *Course of Study* of 1907 enumerated state aims for the schools, among them: to furnish an outline of various subjects areas "in accordance with established and approved methods," to help "advance the pupil through school life . . . thereby lessening the evil effects of a too-frequent change of teachers," and to better inform parents and school board members about "what the schools are accomplishing for their children" (5).

Brief snippets from this Kansas Course (1907) help give the flavor of these standards. From fourth-grade arithmetic, fourth month, for example: "Teach the 4's of the multiplication tables. Teach to count by 4. Teach to multiply by 2; by 3. Continued drill in addition and subtraction. Give thorough drill in the use of all fractions given in the text." For fourth-grade arithmetic, fifth month: "Emphasize analysis, both oral and written" (44). Despite the detailed specifications, the Kansas (1907) state superintendent insisted that administrative oversight was not intended to be excessive. "Great care has been taken not to encroach upon the individuality of the teacher," he wrote. "In general, the Course states what matter should be taught and the order of teaching successive subjects; to the teacher is left *how* to teach them" (5).

A glimpse of one conversation among practitioners illustrates how attitudes continued to be mixed about the appropriate role for state leadership in education. In an 1890 address to the National Education Association (NEA), William Maxwell, school superintendent of Brooklyn, New York, worried that the Brooklyn schools had "no uniform standard" that all students should attain, and consequently, he said, many children left school "before they acquire the minimum of knowledge which every citizen should possess" (City School Systems, 1890: 452–453 [hereafter, City Systems]).

According to Maxwell, it was the state that "should determine the course of study to be pursued in all its public schools. It should determine the minimum amount of knowledge necessary for citizenship. It should fix the subjects of study and their proper sequence, and it should fix the minimum amount of time per week to be devoted to each subject." The state, not his disruptive municipal school board members, could "command the services of the most scientific thinkers and most expert educators to formulate a course of study. . . . Where there is not a uniform course of study," Maxwell concluded, "a common standard cannot be established." (City Systems, 1890: 452–453).

Not all superintendents of the time agreed with Maxwell. The superintendent of Providence, Rhode Island, worried that the type of centralized state control Maxwell advocated was "unnecessary and injurious." "Let us have the unity" that stems from experience, he said, "not that rigid uniformity that comes from external prescription" (City Systems, 1890: 461).

Superintendent H. S. Jones of Erie, Pennsylvania, was troubled by Maxwell's assumption that the people of the United States were homogenous. Far from it, Jones reminded his colleagues. "One of the marked weaknesses of the public school system today is its stubborn tendency toward uniformity in courses of study . . . instruction and management." Jones called for "elasticity, and even wide differences" between schools (City Systems, 1890: 461).

"Too often," Jones said, "city school systems bury expert talent under a grinding service in details that could as well be handled by persons of ordinary ability. . . . The expert teacher must be called from the tread-mill of routine and set at the solution of the hundreds of problems which stand as obstructions to genuine progress" (City Systems, 1890: 464–465).

## THE PROGRESSIVE ERA, 1890s–1940s

The Progressive Era marked a crucial turning point in the history of American education. In the 1890s a common curriculum remained the goal of many leaders, but by 1920 that goal had shifted dramatically; in fact, educators essentially reversed course.

Around the turn of the century observers generally found a fair amount of uniformity, especially among city schools, probably because urban districts frequently sought to ensure compliance through strict supervision of classroom practices. Yet, when taken to extremes, educational uniformity could become stultifying, rigid, and inhumane. Such was the situation encountered by pediatrician Joseph Rice in 1891 when he inspected schools in New York City.

To his dismay, Rice (1893) found classroom cultures antithetical to healthy learning. Rice vividly described classrooms that enforced silence, immobility, and rote learning. He decried that pupil exercises were "still conducted on the antiquated notion that the function of the school consists primarily, if not entirely, in crowding into the memory of the child a certain number of cut-and-dried facts." "Consequently," said Rice, "the aim of the instruction is limited mainly to drilling facts into the minds of children, and to hearing them recite lessons that they have learned by heart from textbooks" (20). Throughout the 1890s Rice and other critics found similar conditions in other urban schools across the nation.

Not until the early twentieth century did educators begin to fully face the consequences of the excesses of nineteenth-century standardization. By 1904 Maxwell (the Brooklyn superintendent discussed above) had become superintendent of the newly centralized New York City public school system, and he soon uncovered distressing evidence that thousands of children weren't learning the required knowledge and skills from the standard curriculum. In many classrooms teachers found themselves with an abundance of older children accumulating in the lower grade levels, unable to pass the promotion exams required to advance to the next grade.

Maxwell published statistics showing that 39 percent of students were above the normal age for their grades, and his report sent a jolt through the educational world. Other investigators set out to discover the reasons for these distressing failures. Leonard Ayres, a researcher with the Russell Sage Foundation, found similar situations in cities in Tennessee, North Carolina, and Utah, and, in fact, in most states across the nation. In other words, New York was no anomaly.

Ayres (1909) ultimately concluded that the popular educational practices of the day were unjust to the child and disastrous to the schools. "Our courses of study as at present constituted," he asserted, "are fitted not to the slow child or to the average child but to the unusually bright one" (4). The nineteenth-century curriculum, they said, was too academic, uniform, and outdated.

However, Ayres voiced a second sentiment that was also gathering increasing credence at the time: most American pupils, he felt, were simply incapable of learning the standard subject matter. This explanation immediately appealed to many educators for two reasons. First, it explained the accumulation of so many failures. Second, and more consequentially, it effectively placed the blame for these failures on the students themselves, rather than on the schools. Such an approach gained widespread approval once IQ tests were introduced following World War 1.

The resulting solution was to divide the once-common curriculum into several *different* curricula, each targeting a separate student ability level. Many reformers believed this offered a straightforward solution to the problems facing urban school systems, for it delivered distinct kinds of coursework to children who had been classified according to their different ability levels, backgrounds, and projected futures and career paths (i.e., "tracking").

Tracking completely overturned the logic of the nineteenth century and signaled a new era in the treatment of school children. Equal *opportunity* became the focus of progressive democracy, and according to educational leaders, "opportunity" entailed discarding the old practices of the common curriculum and instead diversifying the Course of Study. This shift, from *equal curriculum* to *equal opportunity*, marked one of the most important turning points in the conception of American democratic education.

Nevertheless, even as districts differentiated their curricula and used tests to classify children into ability groups, many leaders still attempted to identify the core academic knowledge and skills that all students should learn. After all, schools still had to turn children into functioning citizens, so what was the baseline amount of curricular content that all students should receive? Between 1892 and 1918 national leaders appointed a series of committees charged with determining the kinds of subject matter to which all students should be exposed.

The first of these was the Committee of Ten (1893), established in part to determine what students should learn during their years in secondary school. The committee addressed a set of questions, some of which still hold pertinence today; for example: "Should students going to college receive the same education as those who would go directly into the workforce?" Ultimately, the committee concluded that "every subject which is taught at all in a secondary school should be taught in the same way and to the same extent to every pupil so long as he pursues it, no matter what the probable destination of the pupil may be, or at what point his education is to cease" (17). In retrospect, the committee's report seems the very embodiment of egalitarian statements on American secondary education, but it was ultimately much less influential than the rising breed of "scientists" who pushed for testing and tracking.

Other attempts to determine "minimum essentials" for all students followed. Starting in 1911 under the auspices of the NEA's "Committee on the Economy of Time in Education," scholars set out to answer question such as: "What subjects are essential constituents of the elementary curriculum?" and "What is the absolutely essential content in each subject?" Most of these studies resulted in recommendations for specific "objective standards" in reading, writing, spelling, arithmetic, history, and geography, among other core subjects (Wilson, 1915: 14). Despite such investigations, most educational leaders settled for a regime of testing and tracking that persisted for decades; few stopped to consider why so many poor and minority students were consistently consigned to the lowest tracks.

## 1950s–1970s: TWO PARALLEL MOVEMENTS

As we saw with the transition from the Common School Era into the Progressive Era, the reforms and solutions of one time period often become new educational problems for the next generation. A similar pattern emerged in the 1950s, but this time two distinct groups of reformers offered sharply contrasting views of American education. The first was Arthur Bestor, a historian who launched an attack on public schools in his book *Educational Wastelands*.

Bestor (1953) and others like him, charged schools with dethroning intellectual values and lowering the aims of education. Bestor placed the blame at the feet of progressives; his solution was to return to the kind of liberal education that would offer a "more rigorous standard" (7). When the Soviet Union launched its satellite Sputnik into space in October 1957, well ahead of any comparable American space effort, it seemed to confirm what critics had complained about for nearly a decade: the United States was falling behind its international rivals.

In fact, the year after Sputnik, *Life* magazine (1958) ran a series of articles charging just that. There was a "Crisis in Education," *Life*'s cover story claimed: "There is no general agreement on what the schools should teach. . . . Most appalling, the standards of education are shockingly low" (25). The result of this national turmoil was the passage of the National Defense Education Act of 1958 (NDEA), which among other things offered federal assistance to improve the teaching of math and science.

The second major effort of the period, one that paralleled the excellence movement, offered a strikingly different perspective on the educational challenges of the 1950s and 1960s: the Civil Rights Movement. Civil rights activists drew attention to the scandalous treatment of African American children, the dreadfulness of segregated schooling, and—once integration commenced—the shunting of poor and minority children into the lowest tracks and worst schools. To civil rights leaders the problems of American education appeared much more serious than low standards in the white suburban schools that *Life* had profiled.

If NDEA represented the federal response to the perceived academic weaknesses symbolized by Sputnik, then the Elementary and Secondary Education Act of 1965 (ESEA) was the federal counterpart targeting equity. However, it wasn't until the ESEA reauthorizations of 1988 that the federal government began to address both equity and high standards in tandem.

## THE 1980s AND BEYOND

As noted above, the 1980s are usually depicted as the point of origin for more recent histories of standards, and not without reason. After *A Nation at Risk*, a flurry of activity yielded numerous graduation requirements, escalated certification requirements for teachers, and more attention to core academic subjects.

Without recognizing that they were essentially replicating efforts of early twentieth-century educators, national leaders proposed and launched committees to determine the knowledge that all kids should know. Some panels were created by legislative action, others by state governors, and yet others by public-private partnerships. They included the National Center on Education and the Economy (1988), the National Council on Education Standards and Testing (NCEST) (1991), and the National Education Goals Panel (1993). NCEST nicely distilled the general goals of the 1990s when it explicitly stated that it was not proposing a national curriculum, but that it hoped to set in motion mechanisms that would "result in *local* commitment to high *national* expectations for achievement for all students" (NCEST, 1992: ii).

We should recognize, however, that interpretations of "local commitment" and state or national "expectations" have often varied greatly, sometimes leading to the imposition of particular curricular approaches. As we have seen, however, leaders at the state level, if not at the district or school levels, have often sought to remind practitioners that standards need not be implemented rigidly, nor must they reduce instructional flexibility. Other chapters in this volume cover the most recent reform efforts, but it might be pointed out that one reason that NCLB and CCSS have received widespread, often bipartisan, support is that advocates have portrayed both initiatives as addressing the two overriding concerns of the past half century: equity and excellence. By seeking rigorous standards that all pupils should attain, these efforts have returned to a concept that has been out of fashion for over a century: uniform, high-quality standards for all American schoolchildren.

## CONCLUSION

As this history illustrates, practitioners and leaders have long sought to define the kinds of knowledge and skills they want schoolchildren to attain. By properly attuning our ears to the recurrence of historical themes, we have seen standards established for a range of reasons.

Americans have expected standards to resolve some of the thorniest challenges in American education. Among these have been efforts to: unify a diverse nation, provide greater equity, enhance professionalization, dampen discord among layers of the system, save money, offer accountability, ensure student learning and greater achievement, provide a hedge against teacher turnover, and spark conversation among teachers, administrators, home, and school.

Yet educators have also worried about the potential unintended consequences of emphasizing standards, including: overcentralization, excessive standardization, stripping teachers of their expertise, stifling teacher creativity and innovation, and setting benchmarks that are either too high or too low. Finding an appropriate balance between state uniformity and local liberty has always proven difficult, and it is likely to remain an ongoing project. Therefore, rather than hope this tension will resolve itself or dissolve, a better approach might be to confront it head on.

With that in mind, this chapter comes to a close with questions that emerge out of this history, queries that might be productively explored between and among teachers, administrators, and policymakers, in hopes of stimulating discussion:

1. Do common expectations necessarily stifle teacher freedom, innovation, and creativity? How and when should instructional originality be encouraged?
2. Does commonality inevitably lead to uniformity and standardization? Or can it be used to provide equal educational opportunities to all students?
3. How might we treat the standards as the beginning of a conversation between and among teachers, parents, administrators, and students, rather than a way of ending discussion?

## Chapter Fourteen

# Core Confusion

*A Practitioner's Guide to Understanding Its Complicated Politics*

Patrick McGuinn

Advocates of the Common Core State Standards (CCSS) believe that high, uniform academic standards are essential to improving the academic performance of American students, better preparing them for college and careers, and increasing their—and our nation's—ability to compete in the global marketplace. They argue that the uneven and generally low expectations for student learning in previous state standards, along with the misalignment of state tests to state standards, has been a major obstacle to education reform in the United States. In tandem with "next-generation assessments" that will provide more meaningful information about student progress than earlier multiple-choice tests, the hope is that the Core will promote "twenty-first century skills" and serve as the foundation for robust, data-driven instruction and improved accountability systems.

However, surveys of teachers and the general public have found growing opposition to the Common Core as it entered its first year of full implementation nationwide in 2014/2015. These same surveys have also found that most people do not know much (if anything) about the Common Core and that much of what they think they know is incorrect. It is important to understand that opposition to the Core does not stem from a single source and is not confined to members of one political party. There are many different reasons why people dislike the Common Core, and it is important to disaggregate the different *sources* of opposition and to dispel some of the myths that have swirled around it. This is crucial to understanding the unusual political alliances that have emerged during Core implementation and how the politics of the Core are likely to play out over the longer term.

## FEDERAL AND PRESIDENTIAL OVERREACH

Some, particularly Tea Party adherents and others on the right, view the CCSS as a dangerous (and even unconstitutional) expansion of federal control into education and a violation of states' rights. The word "education" does not appear in the U.S. Constitution, and our country has a strong tradition of local control of schools. Beginning with the passage of No Child Left Behind (NCLB) in 2001, the federal role in education has grown tremendously, and like the law itself, has become more controversial. The CCSS originated from—and continues to be led by—the National Governors Association and the Council of Chief State School Officers—not the federal government. But the Obama administration's use of the Race to the Top (RTT) grant competition and NCLB waiver application process to encourage states to adopt the standards—and its funding of the two consortia that developed the aligned assessments—have raised new concerns that Uncle Sam is becoming a national schoolmarm. This involvement—along with the Obama administration's vocal support for the Core—has made it easy for opponents to cast it as a federal initiative. It is a claim that, while erroneous, is believed by a majority of Americans who have heard of the Common Core: The 2014 *Education Next* survey found that 64 percent believe that "the federal government requires all states to use the Common Core standards."

As a result, the Common Core has become a powerful and threatening symbol of big government to conservatives. Conservative dislike of a Democratic president and the Affordable Care Act ("Obamacare") has been transferred to the Common Core ("Obamacore"). There is an interesting parallel between 2014 and 1994 in this regard: Both periods featured a Democratic president (Obama and Clinton) facing a Republican House majority in the wake of a major health care reform push. Then, as now, national education standards (called Goals 2000 in 1994) became a symbol of ideological opposition to big government. Once championed by conservatives, national standards have now become identified as a "liberal" policy and an "Obama" policy and become a major target for Tea Party members in particular. A number of conservative organizations (such as Freedom Works, American Principals Project, and the Pioneer Institute) have found opposition to the Common Core to be a very successful way to attract new members and donations. Republican candidates for state and federal office seized on the issue during the 2014 elections as a way of mobilizing the GOP base. And some Republicans contemplating a 2016 presidential bid—including Louisiana governor Bobby Jindal, a former Core supporter—are highlighting their opposition to the Common Core as a way to appeal to the more conservative voters who dominate GOP primaries.

## POST-NSA FEARS ABOUT DATA MINING AND PRIVACY

The Common Core had the great misfortune to emerge on the public agenda in the wake of the revelations of widespread privacy violations by the National Security Agency. The centralized collection of student information and test scores at the heart of the Common Core thus collided with heightened fears about data mining. In this context, conspiracy theorists like Michelle Malkin could whip up public fear with her *National Review* column "Common Core as Trojan Horse: It's Time to Opt out of the Creepy Federal Data-Mining Racket." As a result, the 2014 *Education Next* survey found that 85 percent of Americans who have heard of the Common Core believe (erroneously) that the federal government will receive detailed data on individual students' test performance. While the federal government has funded the development of longitudinal state databases of student performance information, there are no data collection or reporting requirements connected to the Common Core, and the federal government will not have access to any of the individual student information that states choose to collect.

## BIG BUSINESS, CORPORATE REFORM, AND PRIVATIZATION

Some of the opposition to the Common Core is related to a broader pushback against the standards, testing, and accountability movement, which has been dubbed "corporate school reform" by critics on the left. The business community has been one of the most vocal supporters of the Common Core, arguing that higher academic standards are imperative to ensuring that the American economy has the high-quality workforce necessary to compete in the global marketplace. The Business Roundtable and the Chamber of Commerce—along with major corporations such as Exxon-Mobil, Intel, and Time Warner Cable—have funded pro–Common Core advocacy campaigns. Microsoft founder Bill Gates has been a vocal supporter as well, and his foundation has contributed a great deal of money to the cause. The association of big business with the Core at a time of historically unprecedented corporate political contributions and enormous economic inequality has activated Americans' long-standing fear of a power elite that dictates government policy over the masses.

Some have argued that the Core is really a scheme intended to increase the profits of the big textbook providers (such as Pearson), education tech companies (such as Microsoft), or test-makers (such as the College Board). Still others see the Core as part of an even larger conspiracy to dismantle public schools and privatize education entirely. In this view, public schools will struggle to meet the higher standards—and not receive the resources with which to do so—and this will open the door to the expansion of charter schools, private school voucher programs, and online virtual learning.

## CURRICULUM AND THE CULTURE WARS

The crafting of new national standards has also reignited long-standing ideological debates (the "curriculum wars") about multiculturalism, how American literature and history should be taught, and whether the teaching of science should or should not include reservations about evolution and global warning. Opponents of the Core cast it as a national curriculum—anathema in a country with such religious, political, ethnic, and cultural diversity. There is a concern among conservatives that progressive educators attempt to use the public schools to indoctrinate children with liberal social and economic values on such hot-button issues as homosexuality, abortion, sex education, and socialism, and these fears have been stoked by a national standards movement pushed by a Democratic president.

The standards outline the essential skills and information that students should know in math and language arts but do not mandate a particular curriculum for delivering instruction, and states are free to add to what is included in the Core. Core advocates, however, have endeavored in vain to communicate that standards are not curriculum—another distinction (like federal versus national and standards versus assessments) that the general public has had a difficult time understanding. In addition, many opponents of the Core believe it mandates particular textbooks or pieces of literature; while it does not, the authors of the standards have recommended a list of materials that have been judged to satisfy the Core. Nonetheless this is another area where public misperception is driving down support for the Core, as only half of Americans who have heard of it understand that states and local school districts retain the ability to choose their own educational materials under the new standards (2014 *Education Next* survey).

## ANTI-TESTING BACKLASH

Other opposition to the CCSS—particularly among parents—is related to a broader backlash against the amount of testing—and teaching to the test—that students are perceived to be facing in the wake of NCLB. While the Core standards are separate from the new assessments (and states can and have adopted one but not the other) they have become conflated in the public mind, and so concerns about testing have spilled over into the push for common academic expectations. While proponents argue that the Common

Core standards and assessments are designed to be an improvement on NCLB (and address many of its failings), many have come to see the Common Core as simply NCLB 2.0.

## MEETING THE HIGHER BAR

The debate over the Common Core has also become entangled with long-standing concerns—prominently articulated by Diane Ravitch and Linda Darling-Hammond, among others—that governments are not doing enough to address the impact of poverty and outside-of-school problems on student achievement and that teachers are not being given sufficient training and resources with which to effectively instruct disadvantaged students. Civil rights and anti-poverty groups, while supportive of the effort to raise expectations for students, are concerned about the impact of the harder assessments on disadvantaged students' K–12 progression and whether adequate resources will be devoted to remediation. In particular, there is a fear that poor performance on the new, more rigorous assessments might lead to even more poor and minority kids being held back from advancing to the next grade or from passing exit exams and receiving a diploma, thus exacerbating already large racial and socioeconomic achievement gaps.

## INTERTWINED WITH NEW TEACHER AND PRINCIPAL EVALUATION SYSTEMS

Teachers and school administrators and their unions were initially quite supportive of Common Core and its potential to improve teaching and learning. They have become increasingly concerned, however, that states have tied new teacher and principal evaluation systems to the new standards and assessments too quickly, before the kinks in the new systems have been ironed out. They fear that this will result in arbitrary or unfair personnel decisions. A 2014 Gallup poll found that 76 percent of teachers continue to support the goals of the Common Core, but only 27 percent support using computerized tests to measure student performance, and only 9 percent support using those test scores to evaluate teachers. Teachers and principals are the most frequent—and most respected—communicators with parents, so their concerns have likely been passed along. The U.S. Department of Education is permitting states to delay the use of student achievement data in the new evaluations; and in states that have chosen to do so, this will likely help to disconnect the two reforms, at least in the short term.

# PROBLEMATIC IMPLEMENTATION BY STATES AND DISTRICTS

State education agencies and districts are struggling to finance and manage the implementation of new standards and assessments, and this is generating strong pushback in some states that the effort is proceeding too quickly and needs to be slowed down. States have varied widely in how well they have implemented the Common Core and the aligned assessments and how effectively they have communicated with educators, parents, and the general public about this work. Implementation problems have led to political pushback in places such as New York, where critics cited insufficient preparation for teachers and parents. Governor Cuomo called the state's rollout of the standards "flawed," and the New York affiliate of the National Education Association withdrew its support until "major course corrections" take place. Tennessee and Kentucky, on the other hand, are widely praised for their implementation and communication work, and (as Jennifer O'Day describes in her chapter in this book) California developed a comprehensive program of supports funded by a $1.25 billion grant that included stakeholder engagement, teacher preparation, and statewide field testing of the new Smarter Balanced Assessment Consortium (SBAC) test.

There was widespread recognition of the need to prepare the public for spring 2015 when the new tests were given for the first time nationwide, and for the release of the test scores, given that most experts expected the harder tests to result in a significant score drop. Kentucky, for example, reached out to educate their media around what they called "the new baseline." However, given that recent surveys have found that a majority of Americans have never even heard of the Common Core, it does not appear that the communication efforts have been successful in most places.

## ADVOCATES HAVE STRUGGLED TO COMMUNICATE

Much of the opposition to the Common Core is based on misinformation or misunderstanding. Advocates have struggled to cut through all of the noise to explain to the general public—and even the media—what the Common Core is and what it is not, and to articulate a clear, consistent, and convincing rationale for how it will improve American education. Common Core advocates also failed to anticipate the political backlash and to respond to it in a rapid or coordinated manner. There were several reasons for this. First, the speed and process by which states adopted the Common Core, and the way it was pushed through the Race to the Top application process, meant it all happened largely under the radar—without much public discussion or debate. Common Core proponents focused initially on communicating with political elites in order to get the Core adopted and to protect it from repeal attempts in state legislatures. They then focused on communicating with teachers and administrators to assist with their implementation work. Advocates did not turn their attention to educating the public about the Common Core until much later and, as a result, allowed opponents to define the Core (negatively) for too long. They have also struggled to address the many different sources of opposition to the standards described earlier in this chapter and the fact that there are critics on both the left and the right.

Common Core advocates have also struggled to combat the volume and speed of opponents' messaging on social media where information (and misinformation) is being disseminated rapidly and widely, often unbeknownst to proponents. The concentration of so much of the communication activity on social media has also made it difficult to identify and measure the amount or intensity of opposition. In addition, research by Daly, Supovitz, and del Fresno (discussed elsewhere in this volume) has shown that a handful of individuals are creating many groups and most of the content, and that there is no real debate over the standards or communication between supporters and opponents; instead, social media is serving as an echo chamber in which opponents are talking to opponents and supporters to supporters. Common Core advocates have also been challenged by the tremendous turnover among governors, legislators, and state superintendents—many of the folks who initially made the decision to adopt the Core are no longer in office and have been replaced by folks who are less supportive or less invested in its success. This problem was exacerbated by the November 2014 elections, and this turnover came at the worst possible time for the Core—in the middle of the first year of full implementation and testing for states.

Much of the communications work that has been done by Core proponents has been passive or reactive. It has been passive in the sense that while a lot of advocacy groups developed informational materials, tool kits, and websites that touted the benefits of the Common Core, they often didn't actively push that message out into schools and communities. Much of the messaging was also reactive—responding to attacks on the Core rather than proactively making the case for it. Oddly, the leaders of colleges and universities—who are supposed to be among the prime beneficiaries of the Core's focus on college and career readiness—remained largely silent during the backlash.

Apparently there was not clarity about whose job it was to communicate on behalf of the Common Core. The standards were created by the National Governors Association and the Council of Chief State School Officers, but as member organizations with small staffs they are not really equipped or culturally inclined to engage in large-scale communication work with the general public. Messaging fell by default to state departments of education, which have their own capacity issues and tend to be staffed by technocrats, and they developed a technocratic message that fell on deaf ears. Advocates have struggled to combat the passionate ideological rhetoric of opponents like Glenn Beck and Michelle Malkin with reasoned arguments about the benefits of the Core.

Similarly the two assessment consortia (Partnership for Assessment of Readiness for College and Careers [PARCC] and SBAC) have really focused their attention and resources on addressing the technical issues surrounding the design, piloting, and full implementation of the new assessments. They do not see it as their job to defend the assessments or standards politically. In general, the national organizations seem to feel that the communication work should be done by state and local folks, while the state and local folks feel that it should be the responsibility of the national organizations, in part because of limited capacity. In addition, the particular arguments being made against the Common Core (and the groups making them) vary widely from state to state, making it difficult to develop a single response. The staff at state and district education agencies were also reportedly so busy actually doing the demanding work of implementing the Common Core and new assessments that they didn't have time to defend the work.

## CONCLUSION

The Common Core has become a proxy for a wide variety of issues swirling around in education debates and in American politics more broadly. As the research of Daly, Supovitz, and del Fresno shows (www.hashtag commoncore.com), Twitter activity around the Core is frequently connected to anger at President Obama, secretary of education Arne Duncan, testing, Bill Gates, and the federal government. The multitude of reasons fueling opposition to the Core—as well as the ideological diversity of opponents—will likely preclude a sustained political alliance or agreement on an alternate vision for American education that can compete with the Core.

The longer that states have adopted the Common Core standards, the less likely they will drop them. State governments, school administrators, and teachers have already invested a tremendous amount of time, effort, and money in implementing the Core and realigning their education systems around the new standards and assessments. These represent "sunk costs" that cannot be recouped if a state changes direction, and the replacement of the Core with something truly new would require significant new investment to develop. As a result, states are likely to become increasingly "path depen-dent" with regard to the Core as time goes on. These dynamics mean that large numbers of states are unlikely to repeal the Core and that even in those states that do, many (like Indiana and Pennsylvania) are likely to simply rename the standards or readopt a slightly modified version. As we have already seen, however, it is more likely that states will pull out of the two major assessment consortia (PARCC and SBAC), which may ultimately constrain the impact that the new standards can have on American education.

Despite all of the different sources of opposition to the Common Core described above, two points should be emphasized. First, most Americans have never heard of the Core, and those who have heard of it tend to know little about it and hold many misperceptions about what it does and does not do. Second, while the Common Core "brand" has been damaged, surveys show that support for the idea of national standards remains strong among teachers and the general public. As a result, if the misconceptions about the Core can be cleared up—and the argument for why it is a good thing for American education communicated more effectively—much of the opposition is likely to dissipate.

*Chapter Fifteen*

# Implementation Politics and the Common Core

## Kathryn A. McDermott

It seems like the politics are over once a new idea has officially become a policy. However, implementation of policies has its own kind of politics. Putting policies into practice can reopen earlier disagreements and spark new ones.

This chapter explains how political scientists and policy researchers think about politics and policy implementation, and offers ideas for maintaining perspective while standing in the middle of the three-ring political circus.

## YOU CAN'T KEEP POLITICS OUT OF POLICY IMPLEMENTATION

Educators have been trying for a century or more to insulate public schools from politics. Nobody likes the idea of the textbook budget being siphoned off into a politician's slush fund, or wants their kids' teachers to have gotten their jobs by working on somebody's political campaign.

But not all politics is about corruption. It helps to think in terms of "big-P" and "small-p" politics. Big-P politics are the things that often make us cringe, like partisanship, cronyism, and the power of big money. If you read works by political theorists, you'll discover another definition of politics, linked to all the difficult, though important, decisions that have to be made whenever a community tries to do something together. This is what I call "small-p" politics—or what a popular policy analysis textbook describes as "people fighting over what the public interest is and trying to realize their own definitions of it" (Stone, 2002: 21).

Discussing public education inevitably requires weighing competing priorities and values. Political debates also are about power: who should be able to make which decisions, and to whom those decision makers should be accountable. Although it's easy to assume that implementing a policy or program is just a matter of doing whatever the policy or program says to do, implementing policy is also a fundamentally "small-p" political process. This is because all of the things that the policy designers left ambiguous have to become concrete when a policy actually goes into action.

For example, in 1993 the Massachusetts state legislature enacted an education reform law that required the state to have a "system of assessments" that "as much as practicable" should include "consideration of work samples, projects, and portfolios" (Massachusetts General Laws, chapter 69, section 1I). The law also called for a "Competency Determination" as a condition for earning a high school diploma (Commonwealth of Massachusetts, Acts and Resolves of 1993, chapter 71, section 68).

While the legislature was considering the law, its members could interpret words like "system of assessments" and "practicable" in different ways, and this ambiguity helped get the law passed. Later, the state's board of education had to decide what a "system of assessments" was and whether it was "practicable" to include anything other than tests. Once the board decided that the assessment system would consist only of standardized tests, it then had to decide how high a student needed to score in order to earn a high school diploma. Making these decisions meant setting priorities among competing values, with the knowledge that the ultimate decision would have real effects on students' lives.

At this point, the testing issue became far more controversial than it had been when the law passed. Legislators could have had various things in mind when they agreed to support a "system of assessments" and a "competency determination," but the concrete reality of a test with a passing score did not produce the same consensus. In addition, the decision represented a major increase in the state government's power over local school districts. Implementing the competency determination made this shift more obvious than it had previously been.

**Why this matters:** Understanding that implementation has unavoidable political dimensions may not make the process less exhausting, but it does help put it into perspective. Doing something new is just about guaranteed to bring questions about values, priorities, and material interests to the surface, within the community as well as among people who work in schools. It may feel like people are refighting old battles, but from their perspective, the battles seem quite new.

## THE COMMON CORE CHANGES OTHER STANDARD OPERATING PROCEDURES FOR EDUCATION POLICY, AND THESE CHANGES HAVE POLITICAL CONSEQUENCES

What was just said about small-p politics in policy implementation is especially true of the CCSS. To develop the standards, state governments and national organizations worked together in new ways. The standards and tests also represent major changes in the relationship between federal and state governments and between public and private organizations in education.

Sharing the same standards across nearly the whole nation, and using the same test in as many as two dozen states, are both new ideas. The closest thing to a precedent for it is the New England Common Assessment Program (NECAP), in which Maine, New Hampshire, Rhode Island, and Vermont jointly developed tests for No Child Left Behind (NCLB) accountability. With NECAP, the four states' policymakers found that they liked the common test better than what they'd started with, and that they were paying less for this better test because they were sharing the costs of test development (McDermott, 2013).

NECAP required huge investments of time by staff of the four states' departments of education, as they hashed out questions like whether or not students should be allowed to use calculators. In making these decisions, it helped a lot that these states are small and close together, which made face-to-face meetings feasible. Face-to-face meetings built trust, which was particularly important because NECAP required state officials to share authority over testing.

NECAP also didn't fit neatly into how states were used to doing business with private companies. State contracting laws are based on the idea that the state will solicit bids from multiple companies and choose the one that delivers the best value. In particular, states can't legally collude with a particular supplier to develop a set of specifications that only that supplier's bid will meet. These laws are intended to prevent "sweetheart" deals and other forms of corruption.

When the original three NECAP states (Vermont, New Hampshire, and Rhode Island) chose a contractor to develop the test, they had to work together behind the scenes in order to follow their states' separate contracting laws while still making the decision together. The state officials worked together to decide which proposal to accept, negotiated together with Measured Progress, the chosen contractor, and issued separate but identical contracts. Trust developed through face-to-face interactions which made it possible for the states to do something that did not fit neatly into their existing laws about government contracts. The states' officials trusted that the process would stay true to the letter and spirit of these laws (McDermott, 2013:147).

PARCC and SBAC, the two large, multistate consortia that have been working on assessments for the CCSS, face challenges on a much larger scale. More states are involved, which means more relationships to be developed. In this more complicated environment, it's intrinsically harder to reach consensus, and harder to rely on trust and gentlepersons' agreements.

In addition, the CCSS differ from individual states' standards and tests in that they came out of a network of organizations rather than a single government body. The National Governors Association and the Council of Chief State School Officers (CCSSO) jointly launched the Common Core State Standards Initiative (CCSSI) in early 2009. The CCSSI has had financial support from the Bill and Melinda Gates Foundation and the Hewlett Foundation, among others. The governors and state school chiefs wanted the benefits of shared standards, but they also did not want those standards to come from the federal government. The federal role in public education has long been controversial, and in the 1990s conflict was particularly intense over voluntary national standards.

For people who liked the idea of national standards, the CCSSI process neatly sidestepped the toxic politics around federal government involvement. The idea began in national organizations that represented state officials, and states could decide whether or not to participate. The CCSS do not belong to any government entity. The National Governors Association Center for Best Practices and the Council of Chief State School Officers (CCSSO) hold the copyright on the standards.

However, the U.S. Department of Education (USED) has blurred the line between state-developed shared standards and federal policy. First, it awarded extra points to Race to the Top applications from states that were using shared, internationally benchmarked standards. The CCSS are the only such standards. All Race to the Top winning states had adopted the CCSS, though not all states that adopted the CCSS won Race to the Top funds. Second, USED made $350 million in grants to the two consortia developing CCSS-aligned assessments.

Later, USED required states seeking No Child Left Behind waivers either to adopt shared, internationally benchmarked standards or to demonstrate that they had standards for college and career readiness that had been approved by their state higher education systems. Some states that had not adopted the CCSS got NCLB waivers; however, Oklahoma lost its waiver when it dropped the CCSS (Camera, 2014).

Working through a network of states, the CCSSI produced standards that were national in scope though not technically "federal." The idea that a national-scale project like common standards and tests could come from a network of organizations rather than from the federal government is unlikely to make sense to many people at first. Because the federal government set up incentives to adopt the Common Core, like Race to the Top and the NCLB waivers, the CCSSI looks like a federal project rather than a truly voluntary state-led one.

The CCSS also came on the scene at a time when the market for test development had become more highly concentrated, with fewer companies competing. Pearson LLC, which sells both tests and instructional resources, has emerged as the dominant market power.

The CCSS also embody controversial larger changes in education philanthropy. Since the 1990s, educational philanthropy has become more engaged in politics and policy advocacy, more inclined to converge around favored grantees and causes, and more supportive of challenges to traditional educational institutions (Reckhow & Snyder, 2014). The Gates Foundation not only contributed funds to the CCSS development, but also made grants to states so that they could develop stronger Race to the Top applications. The Common Core work of Pearson LLC's nonprofit foundation came under legal attack for advancing the parent company's financial interests. In 2013 Pearson LLC paid New York State $7.7 million to settle a lawsuit (Layton, 2013). In 2014 the Pearson Foundation announced that it was shutting down.

**Why this matters:** All of the new relationships among states and other organizations challenge existing understandings of what it means for government to be accountable to the public. At the same time, because of the federal incentives to participate, the CCSS can also be portrayed as the same old federal coercion in a new form.

Accountability to taxpayers is the underlying goal of laws about government contracts. NECAP's example shows that the mismatch between multistate tests and existing contracting laws is a solvable problem. However, the scale of the Common Core State Standards and the multistate testing consortia dwarfs NECAP. There's nobody to vote out of office if the CCSS get revised in a way that a state's leaders or voters disagree with, or if they aren't revised at all. This challenges basic political accountability.

Although the Pearson Foundation is closing, the Gates Foundation's involvement has been similarly controversial. Schools across the United States are investing in new digital technology so that they can administer the consortia's tests, which are designed to be taken online. Not all of what school districts buy will be Microsoft products, but some will be, and some people believe the Gates Foundation is out to enhance Microsoft's bottom line. Even if everybody's motives are entirely pure, and even though the nonprofit foundation is legally separate from the for-profit company, you don't need to wear a tinfoil hat for the whole setup to seem a bit like a massive conspiracy.

All of this matters for local Common Core implementation because it affects the political environment within which implementation happens. Trust matters, and general goodwill facilitates major changes (as in the NECAP states). If the political environment includes mistrust grounded in questions about whether the private-sector participants in the Common Core are more focused on students' best interests or their own bottom lines, whether Common Core advocates are trying to have things both ways on federal government involvement, or who is accountable and how if the Common Core doesn't work as advertised, then the work will be harder.

## POLICIES RELATED TO THE COMMON CORE ARE MAKING COMMON CORE POLITICS EVEN MORE COMPLICATED THAN THEY'D BE ON THEIR OWN

Survey data indicates that although teachers initially supported the Common Core, that support may be declining (See http://educationnext.org/2014-ednext-poll-no-common-opinion-on-the-common-core/.) It's possible that fewer teachers support the Common Core this year than last year because of the performance accountability policies that surround it—specifically, the push to use students' test scores in teachers' evaluations that has come from Race to the Top and the NCLB waiver requirements.

Under the original version of NCLB, states' choices about how to intervene in lower-performing schools and districts were limited. Adequate Yearly Progress (AYP) goals required higher proportions of students to score proficient each year. The constantly increasing goals meant that states had to sanction more schools and districts each year.

However, the states set their own standards, developed their own tests, and determined their own proficiency standards. Having control over this part of the accountability system provided a way of avoiding having to label most schools and districts as underperforming: States could define "proficiency" as a fairly low level of learning. Many did just that (Reed, 2009). It's not what the authors of NCLB had in mind, but it's an understandable human response.

Although most states now have waivers from the constantly increasing AYP goals of NCLB, the waivers and Race to the Top sustain pressure on teachers and administrators. In addition to the teacher evaluations, schools and districts can still be targeted for state intervention and "turnarounds." Five states implementing the Common Core do not have NCLB waivers, so they still have to follow the original NCLB accountability laws, with constantly rising AYP targets.

The result is likely to be politically messy. Since the tests aligned with the Common Core are actually intended to be harder than many of the tests they are replacing, it is particularly likely that proficiency rates will drop, at least in the short term. Even without any sanctions attached to a teacher's, school's, or district's overall student performance, this would generate some unhappiness. With sanctions, there's pressure for fast improvement. Nobody wants to be identified as low performing, miss out on a possible performance bonus, or lose job security.

**Why does this matter?** In order to realize the possible benefits of the Common Core standards, teachers need to revise curricula and change a great deal of what they are doing every day. This is challenging, intellectually demanding work, and many people get anxious when they are trying to make such big changes in how they do their jobs. Piling on more anxiety about the consequences of failure won't help. As an experienced administrator in my education policy class said recently, "People don't learn well when they're scared."

Although many teachers like the Common Core better than the standards they were using, their fear of what might happen on the basis of their students' test scores undermines both their morale and their implementation of the new standards. For example, New York State's Common Core implementation has been politically intense because the state contracted with Pearson for its own Common Core assessment so that it could begin basing accountability and teacher evaluations on Common Core–defined achievement before the PARCC test was ready. Under pressure to show fast results, teachers in some districts focused on narrowly teaching to the new assessments rather than on implementing the Common Core as it was designed (American Radio Works, 2014).

## POLITICS ON A LARGE SCALE IS INTRINSICALLY DIFFERENT FROM POLITICS ON A SMALL SCALE

In general, state boards of education made the decisions to adopt the Common Core. State boards of education tend to be relatively low-profile decision makers. Usually, members are appointed rather than elected, so they don't campaign and aren't particularly well known. Historically, this is not an accident. Progressive-era good-government reformers created these governing structures that only work on education issues as a way of keeping "politics" out of education policy, and making sure that experts are in charge.

The separate policymaking institutions for education mean that fewer people are involved in making decisions than if the state legislature took them on. In addition to not including extensive public input, many states' adoptions of the Common Core happened on a quick schedule because of the deadline for Race to the Top applications. Peter Meyer of *Education Next* has characterized the Common Core adoptions as flying "under the radar" (Meyer, 2014: 127). According to Meyer, moving quickly and avoiding large-scale political fuss was a deliberate decision, representing a lesson that standards advocates had learned in the 1990s when voluntary federal standards became a national political issue and the efforts fell apart.

**Why does this matter?** When the participants in a debate change, what the debate is about also changes. Political scientist E. E. Schattschneider first made this point in his influential 1960 book, *The Semi-Sovereign People*. The book begins with an account of a fight between two men in Harlem in 1943 that escalated into a riot when bystanders joined in. Schattschneider draws an analogy between fighting and politics, since "the universal lan-guage of conflict" is "at the root of all politics," and conflict is "contagious" (2). Going further, he says that "the way in which the public participates in the spread of the conflict" and "the processes by which the unstable relation of the public to the conflict is controlled" are "at the nub of politics" (3). You can tell that political decision makers care about controlling the spread, or scope, of conflict because of the energy that they put into procedural issues, such as who may vote in an election and how the public must be notified when an official meeting is taking place (8–9).

The CCSS stay-under-the-radar strategy implicitly recognized the power of narrowing the scope of conflict. Flying under the radar kept Common Core decisions predictable. Because the CCSSI began with the National Governors Association and the CCSSO, it came from familiar territory for state board of education members. (State board members generally work closely with their chief state school officers, and many are appointed by their governors.) Knowing that private organizations like Gates and Pearson sup-ported the Common Core would not have alarmed state board members, who have in many cases already approved testing contracts with Pearson or signed off on applications for Gates funding.

However, even when you fly under the radar, eventually you have to land the plane, and it's hard to disguise a jumbo jet on a runway. When public policy changes, people notice, because the point of changing a policy is to change what people do. The increased controversy over the Common Core in the last couple of years comes in part from this increased visibility.

Complicating matters, and further expanding the scope of conflict, a great deal changed in state and national politics shortly after states adopted the CCSS in 2010. In that year's midterm elections, party control of eleven governorships and twelve state legislatures changed from Democrats to Re-publicans. Much of the Republican energy came from conservative candi-dates who were disinclined to trust anything that looked like a federal policy supported by President Obama. The group Utah Republic started calling the CCSS "Obamacore" in 2012, and the idea spread. The Obamacore label links the CCSS to another policy with a less-than-stellar public image.

Conservatives have reframed the controversy over the Common Core as the latest round of the perennially intense controversy about the federal role in education and also linked it to the broader conservative argument that Obama has overstepped the constitutional limits of presidential authority. On the left, because of the Pearson and Gates connections, opposition to the standards has become linked to the fight against increased corporate involvement in public schools.

Schattschneider's story about the one-on-one fight that became a riot shows how the original opponents no longer control what the fight is about once the bystanders have joined in. CCSS advocates initially made technocratic arguments about the quality of the standards and the need for international benchmarking. Now they are in an emotionally charged fight about President Obama, the federal role in education, and corporate power.

Teachers and administrators in schools all over the country are used to seeing the Common Core in terms of its effects in classrooms. The Common Core is not just a set of standards that need to be applied to teaching and learning, though. It represents major changes in how public schools and private organizations interact. It's connected with expanded federal influence over schools, a topic that's guaranteed to be controversial, and it arouses opposition from both the right and left.

Leadership—whether at a district or school level—is deeply political. This includes both the obviously political occasions, like speaking before the school board or other community organization, and smaller-scale moments, like facilitating staff meetings and meeting with parents.

Teachers and other school staff are probably ahead of the general public in their understanding of the Common Core and what it means for their work. They may also be expressing new reservations about the Common Core, either in its own right or as part of a collection of policies that are making their working lives more stressful. Leaders can help staff understand which changes are coming from which sources. It's important to make these distinctions, because some states are now slowing down their schedules for implementing educator evaluation and other changes connected to the Common Core.

If you are a state-level leader and you now have the freedom to extend implementation schedules for the Common Core and related policies, use it. If you work at the local level, take advantage of any relaxing of state accountability timetables to turn down the heat on Common Core politics. (Chapter 16 by Jennifer O'Day explains how California state leaders did this.)

Right now, when leaders hear public complaints about the Common Core, the associated tests, or other policies that people perceive to be connected with the Common Core, it can feel like the people complaining are too late, they should have been paying attention all along, and they should already be better informed about what the Common Core is and is not. From the standpoint of theories about politics and policy implementation, though, these complaints are right on schedule. People with concerns and complaints about the Common Core are surfacing now, not three or four years ago, because now is when the reality of the changes is hitting home.

Since broadening the scope of conflict around the Common Core has thus far weakened support for it, try building support by focusing on the specifics of the standards. In some surveys that show rising public opposition to the "Common Core" when it's identified by name, respondents also express support for the idea of shared, high academic standards. Emphasize the need to prepare all students well for college and careers, and make public whatever evidence you have that your local implementation of the Common Core will accomplish this goal.

People's impressions of the Common Core can be hard to disentangle from their impressions of President Obama, the U.S. Department of Education, or growing corporate power in education policy. Even if you disagree with members of the staff or the public about these other issues that have become entangled with the Common Core as the scope of conflict about it has expanded, it's important to hear them out. Remember that although you may need to convince them to accept how the Common Core is being implemented in your school or district, you do not need to try to change their minds about all of the broader issues. Stick to the relatively uncontested facts about what's in the standards and how the standards are being implemented locally.

Seeing Common Core implementation from a political perspective won't solve whatever practical problems you're dealing with in your school or district. However, it may help you understand what's going on. If politics makes you uncomfortable, you're not alone. However, the "small-p" kind of politics comes up whenever a community faces change and has to make decisions about values and priorities. Recognizing that you can engage in this kind of politics without turning into one of the "large-P" politics characters from *House of Cards* may make the process less uncomfortable.

*Chapter Sixteen*

# A Window of Opportunity

*The Politics and Policies of Common Core
Implementation in California*

## Jennifer A. O'Day

Less than ten years ago, the prospects for California education reform were
bleak. In 2005 a bipartisan group of California leaders commissioned a massive independent investigation of the state's school finance and governance
systems, entitled "Getting Down to Facts" (GDTF). Produced by scholars
from multiple disciplines and research institutions across the country, the
twenty-three reports from this investigation cohered around several core
themes that added up to one overarching conclusion: "California's school
governance and finance systems are fundamentally flawed" (Loeb, Bryk &
Hanushek, 2008: 2). Among the themes were the following: Overregulation
and proliferation of categorical funding streams had led to fragmentation,
contradictory policies, and an emphasis on compliance over effective teaching and learning. Funding for education was sorely inadequate (lagging well
behind national averages, and difficult to increase due to Proposition 13's
constitutional cap on property taxes), unnecessarily complex, and "inequitable by any measure" (6). The state lacked a coherent system for recruiting,
developing, and retaining high-quality teachers and administrators, and it had
neither the data systems nor analytic capacity to enable system learning and
improvement.

Despite their dismal assessment of the then-current situation in the state,
the authors proposed directions for improvement and provided a glimmer of
the possible. But trust was low and political infighting high in the state. The
necessary leadership and action were not forthcoming—and then, less than a
year after the GDTF reports were released, the state plummeted into a severe

fiscal crisis. District budgets were slashed and teachers and administrators were laid off; class sizes soared, and most legislators and education leaders were too busy treading water to see a way forward. By 2010 California ranked dead last in per-pupil expenditures, adjusted for inflation and regional cost of living (Fensterwald, 2014) and had the highest student-teacher ratio of any state in the union (NEA). By 2011 the state had lost two bids for a Race-to-the-Top grant from the American Recovery and Reinvestment Act (ARRA) funds, and even many philanthropic foundations seemed to have given up on the prospect that California could somehow pull itself together enough to lead the fundamental changes necessary.

Yet by 2014 an entirely different policy landscape had taken shape in California. Passage of Proposition 30 in November 2012 brought $6 billion per year in new revenues into state coffers, directed primarily at K–12 and higher education. The Local Control Funding Formula (LCFF) passed in June 2013 has simplified the school finance system, ensured greater equity for targeted student populations across (and hopefully within) school districts, and provided flexibility so that local educators can develop coherent strategies for serving their students and communities. Moreover, stakeholder groups across the state—including the California Teachers Association, state legislators and administrators, higher education and business leaders, advocacy groups, and local educators—have united in support of the Common Core State Standards, and the state legislature allocated an additional $1.25 billion explicitly for CCSS implementation in 2013.

With these and other developments, a window of opportunity has opened up for California education. More specific to the focus of this volume, these policy changes have laid the groundwork for meaningful implementation of the CCSS in the state. This chapter discusses some of the factors that contributed to the emergence of this window, the potential lessons—both for California and for other states and jurisdictions—and the prospects for the future. The underlying premise is that effective CCSS implementation—that is, implementation that actually reaches classroom instruction and opportunities for all students—requires a long-term systemic approach in which policy supports are put in place and relationships among stakeholders are built to create the resources and space needed for the hard work that ultimately rests on schools and teachers.

## WHERE WE STARTED: LOCKED IN A POLICY BOX

Let's begin with a little context. Last year California educated over 6.2 million students, or about one in every eight public school children in the United States. California's students are among the most diverse and disadvantaged in the nation. Approximately 59 percent come from low-income families, compared with 48 percent nationally. [1] Seventy-five percent (75%) are students of color, including 53 percent Hispanics, 9 percent Asian Americans, and 6 percent African Americans, among others. Over 1.4 million, or 23 percent, of the state's students are officially classified as English learners, compared to 9.1 percent nationally (Snyder & Dillow, 2013). California's English learners represent by far the largest number and percent of such students among all U.S. states—indeed, almost one-third of English learners in the United States attend school in the Golden State.

With respect to achievement, California ranked near the bottom among states on the 2013 National Assessment of Educational Progress (NAEP) in reading (47th in grade four and 42nd in grade eight) and mathematics (47th in both grades four and eight). While some observers contend that this low result is due to the disproportionately large numbers of disadvantaged students in the state, the pattern is similar even when we compare scores only within subgroups, particularly low-income and Hispanic students. For example, California students who were eligible for free and reduced-price lunches ranked from 49th (grade four math) to 42nd (grade eight reading) among similarly low-income students in other states. Achievement gaps (between whites and African Americans or Hispanic students and between those eligible and not eligible for the school lunch program) were similar to those nationally, ranging from twenty-five to thirty-three points—or about 2.5 to 3 grade levels across both subjects and grade levels.

Contrary to much of the current reform mythology, responsibility for these poor results should not be laid at the feet of supposedly unmotivated teachers and students. Many teachers and administrators in the state have worked for decades to improve outcomes and opportunities for their students. But too often those efforts have been stymied by a host of policy constraints that have made effective implementation and sustainability difficult to realize, especially at scale.

The finance system prior to 2012 is a prime case in point. This "system" resulted in large part from the accretion of several core policy developments over nearly four decades. These included (a) key equalization court rulings in the 1970s (Serrano I and II), which sought to lessen funding discrepancies across school districts with widely varying tax bases and rates; (b) a massive reduction in property taxes to 1 percent of assessed value, with a 2 percent cap on any future increases (Proposition 13, 1978); and (c) a series of legislative bills (Assembly Bill 8, 1979) and voter propositions (98 and 111 in 1988 and 1990 respectively) that had the combined *intent* of centralizing school funding (increasing the portion from state sources), making it both more predictable and equitable.

Policy intentions are not always policy reality, however. Fiscal equalization à la Serrano did not lead to a truly equitable allocation of resources. Although court rulings limited differences in general revenues per pupil, and centralization of funding sources buffered low-wealth districts, funding formulas did not take into account the varying populations and needs across districts. In addition, many high-wealth communities simply set up foundations to raise additional funds outside the state allocation structure, providing a way around equalization. Nor was funding predictability in intent necessarily predictability in fact. Partisan politics in the legislature, combined with the requirement that lawmakers achieve a two-thirds majority to pass the annual state budget, meant that for twenty years the legislature was simply unable to meet its constitutional obligation to approve a budget by June 15. School districts often did not know how much they would be receiving until right before—or even during—the school year, making planning, preparation, and procurement of needed services and materials difficult. Meanwhile Proposition 13 had significantly reduced all funds available for schools, until California—once among the more supportive of states for education—ranked at or near the bottom with respect to per-pupil expenditures adjusted for inflation and regional differences in cost.

To make matters worse, the finance and governance systems had become bogged down over the years by a proliferation of categorical programs, each with its own interest groups and regulations. Relations between the California Department of Education and school districts were driven by required state monitoring for local compliance with specific and often contradictory programmatic rules and reporting requirements. Districts had to allocate precious staff time and limited financial resources simply to ensure that all the reports' t's were crossed and i's dotted and that state monitoring teams left satisfied that the rules had been followed.

Overregulation not only hampered efficiency, it also thwarted effectiveness, with the result that student performance was significantly lower in districts that received a relatively higher share of their state support in categorical grants, other things being equal (Duncombe & Yinger, 2007). Even in the core academic program, the regulatory state regime took its toll. For example, districts had to adopt textbooks from the approved state list in order to receive any funding for instructional materials. Meanwhile influential forces in the state capital worked to ensure that only certain kinds of highly scripted texts were approved, even when these proved inappropriate for the large EL population or other groups of students requiring differentiated instruction. While some higher-capacity districts were able to avoid the most crippling effects of this state prescription and fragmentation, others were not. Some even mimicked the control modeled at the state level, such that it was not uncommon for teachers in some districts to talk about the "literacy police," referring to district administrators whose task it was to ensure that state-approved literacy programs were implemented with absolute fidelity.

Fragmented, overregulated, and underfunded: This was the state of California's state education system throughout the first decade of the twenty-first century. Although many recognized the problems in the system, politics and an apparently immovable policy structure combined to prevent real change. An important contributor to the situation was California's frequent use of the initiative process, not only to pass new laws but also to put in place amendments to the state constitution (such as Propositions 13, 98, and 111) that could then only be changed through a two-thirds majority vote of the legislature or a subsequent public referendum. Under these conditions, attempts to address the fundamental problems in school finance and governance seemed almost impossible. And without movement on these fronts, all but the most superficial implementation of the new standards would have been unlikely.

## OPENING A POLICY WINDOW

### The Benefits of Adversity

Ironically, stalemates and lack of leadership at the state level, coupled with a deep fiscal crisis, served as unexpected catalysts for opening a window for change. The fiscal crisis had two important effects. It forced the state to temporarily ease up on many of the categorical restrictions, thus providing greater flexibility for districts to make resource-allocation decisions in ways that made sense for their contexts and students. While some districts used this flexibility more effectively than others, the temporary level of discretion nonetheless helped weaken the stranglehold of Sacramento interest groups and pave the way for the transformation of the school finance system that was to follow. Second, the crisis forced districts to severely cut—many would say slash—their already inadequate budgets. In nearly every respect, this was not a good thing. By the time the economic crisis hit in 2008, there was little budgetary fat to cut away. Yet there were still more- and less-effective programs and practices, and some—though not all—districts began incorporating considerations of effectiveness and school need into their fiscal adjustments. Moreover, the leanness of the resulting budgets made room for more reasoned allocation decisions when economic recovery brought more dollars back into district coffers.

Like the dismal fiscal situation, the long-standing lack of state leadership for meaningful improvement also had its positive side. Key districts in the state realized that they could not wait for action at the state level to move forward with policy agendas focused on instructional improvement and equity. They were fortunate to have a few peer systems like Long Beach and Garden Grove that had been making steady improvement for a long time and could demonstrate the possibilities of a continuous focus on students and teachers. Efforts like the Urban Education Dialogue and the California Collaborative on District Reform[2] created ongoing professional communities in which district leaders could learn from one another. In the case of the Collaborative, the social capital (relationships) built among district leaders extended further to include researchers, state policymakers, key philanthropic funders, and even a few leaders from advocacy and support organizations. Lines of communication, cooperation, and collective problem solving that were formed in these ways between 2000 and 2010 helped to underscore the critical role of districts in the improvement/equity equation. They built leadership capacity at the local level as well as understanding across stakeholder groups, thus helping to form the embryonic material from which the current policy emphasis on local discretion could emerge and thrive.

## A Turning Point

The year 2010 became a turning point for California education policy, with the Common Core State Standards (CCSS) serving as an important guide. Indeed, adoption of the CCSS was the first step in what became a four-year whirlwind of policy activity. The adoption process began with the first legislative act of 2010 (Senate Bill 1): authorization of the Academic Content Standards Commission, whose responsibility it was to make a recommendation on college- and career-ready standards to the state board of education before the August deadline for the first round of Race to the Top funding. With input from across the state, the commission recommended and the board approved adoption of the CCSS, with only a few California-specific adjustments. Reflecting on this move and its implications for the state policy structure a short while later, current state board of education president Michael Kirst wrote, "The Common Core changes almost everything."

Those changes started almost immediately, enabled by the gubernatorial election of Jerry Brown in November. Brown had run on a platform focused on reducing California's $20 billion debt through a combination of tax increases for the wealthiest Californians and reduced spending. A longtime friend of education, Brown also sought to break the stranglehold of the state bureaucracy and return greater discretion to local communities and school districts. One of his first acts was to appoint seven Democrats to the state board of education.

Once in place, the new leadership in the state began working through a methodical plan to right the broken education policy system and establish a strong basis for implementation of the Common Core. Much of the activity fell into two broad domains: school finance and support for CCSS-aligned instruction.

## Transforming School Finance and Ensuring Resources for CCSS

Four major policy developments set the fiscal stage for CCSS implementation in the state. First, in the same election that made Jerry Brown governor

(November 2010), voters passed Proposition 25, the On-Time Budget Act of 2010. Fed up with the failure of the legislature to pass the annual budget year after year, Californians did two things in Proposition 25: They eliminated the requirement for a two-thirds majority to approve the state budget and they obliged all legislators to permanently forfeit their salary and expenses for each day they failed to pass a balanced budget after the June 15 deadline. The first of these two provisions removed a key barrier to timely budget action; the second provided an incentive to ensure that action actually occurred. While critics bemoan the continuation of backroom politicking and lack of transparency in the budget process, Proposition 25 was important for education reform by providing the new governor with an unexpected vehicle for transforming the school finance system.

Before that vehicle could be successfully utilized, however, Governor Brown had to address the woefully inadequate level of funding available for education. For this, he turned first to the initiative process, placing on the November 2012 ballot a measure that would levy an income tax increase on the wealthiest 3 percent of Californians, those with incomes above $250,000. This was the second major fiscal policy development. The tax would be temporary, running for seven years, and would be used primarily to fund education and public safety. With broad mobilization of educators, advocates, community and stakeholder organizations, Proposition 30 passed with 55 percent of the vote. This progressive tax was to ameliorate some of the worst of the prior cuts in school districts and to prevent further rollbacks. It also generated needed political capital to push through school finance reform the following spring.

Both the third and fourth developments occurred as part of the 2013/2014 legislative budget process. One of these was a one-time $1.25 billion investment ($200 per student) funneled to school districts to enhance their capacity for CCSS implementation. Districts could spend the money for one or more of three broad categories of activities: professional development, instructional materials developments or adoption, or technology needed for CCSS-aligned instruction and assessment. This action had symbolic as well as material benefits for CCSS implementation, as it demonstrated (a) the continued support of both the governor's office and the state legislature for the Common Core, and (b) a recognition of the critical need for capacity building at the local level if CCSS implementation was to be successful. By requiring a public plan and discourse around the use of the funds, this allocation also provided a kind of trial run for the discretionary decision and planning processes that would go into effect the following spring as part of the Local Control Funding Formula.

The funding formula was the fourth and most transformative of the fiscal policy developments. For years it seemed as though there was no way through the deadlock that is Sacramento politics to push for the needed redesign of the school finance system. But advocates for change had several things going for them in 2013. First, there was an appetite in local communities for greater flexibility and an emergence of leading districts and district partnerships that demonstrated an alternative to the state-dominated structures. Second, even among civil rights groups and long-term advocates of targeted educational programs, there was a growing recognition—backed by the compendium of Getting Down to Facts studies—that the categorical approach was not producing the intended results for underserved students in the state. Third, the fiscal actions outlined above had ameliorated some of the worst of the effects of the Great Recession and allowed people to think about more than defending against the storm. And finally, in Jerry Brown, advocates for change had a champion who was both a supporter of local discretion and a savvy veteran of Sacramento politics.

Brown made a brilliant tactical decision: He would use the budget process streamlined in 2010 by Proposition 25 to push through the transformation rather than getting bogged down in the usual legislative policy process. After an initial abortive attempt to insert a weighted pupil formula into the 2012 budget, Brown and his supporters revised and rebranded the effort as the Local Control Funding Formula in 2013. Stakeholder groups and system leaders across the state—many of whom had been active in efforts to pass Proposition 30—got involved in making recommendations for the changes and in mobilizing very broad constituencies in support of the two fundamental components of the proposed system, both of which are central for CCSS implementation. The first of these was a more equitable and simpler funding formula in which all districts receive a base grant determined by the numbers of students in the various grade spans and supplemented by additional funding weights for unduplicated counts of English language learners, low-income students, and foster youth, as well as for concentrations of these students in the district. The second element was the elimination of nearly all categorical funding streams and the devolution of authority for resource-allocation decisions to the district, rather than state, level. Districts were freed up to use funds in ways that made sense for their local contexts, but they were required to engage their communities in developing local plans. And these plans had to include eight broad state priorities, one of which was implementation of the state's college- and career-ready standards (the CCSS and Next Generation Science Standards).

The fiscal policy activity is given such prominence in this chapter because it was central to state and local capacity to implement the Common Core, and because it involved overlapping constituencies, agencies, and political strategies. But as these activities on the finance front were taking place, shifts were also occurring in policies and structures more directly related to CCSS instruction.

## CCSS Implementation Support Policies

Although many educators and CCSS advocates in the state have criticized the comparative slowness of state efforts around CCSS, initial work in several areas is beginning to bear fruit for stepped-up implementation moving forward. These include the following:

*Curriculum and Instructional Guidance*

Formed in early 2012, the Instructional Quality Commission (IQC) is an advisory body to the state board of education. Under the leadership of former state superintendent Bill Honig, the IQC has developed comprehensive frameworks to assist districts and schools in designing curriculum and instructional approaches aligned to the CCSS standards in mathematics and English language arts (ELA). The ELA/ELD framework incorporates the English language development (ELD) standards adopted by the state board of education in 2013. The commission also reviewed texts and other instructional materials in these two subjects, producing a list of recommended texts in each subject area. An important distinction between this and previous such guidance in the state is that these lists and frameworks are advisory rather than mandatory, as is consistent with the general move toward greater local control.

*Teacher Preparation*

The California Commission on Teacher Credentialing (CTC) has been working to align the subject matter expectations for new teachers and the expectations for teacher preparation programs to the CCSS.

*Higher Education*

All four higher education systems in the state—the University of California, California State University, California Community Colleges, and the Association of Independent California Colleges and Universities—have signed on to the CCSS and have committed themselves in writing to work toward their successful implementation. One reflection of this commitment is the effort underway to revamp the high school course requirements (known as A-G) for admission to any of the UC or CSU campuses so that those requirements align with and support the Common Core.

*Testing and Accountability*

One of the most important steps in support of CCSS implementation was the decision not to administer the California Standards Tests in spring 2014 and instead to expand the field test of the Smarter Balanced Assessment Consortium such that all students in grades three to eight and eleven took the mathematics and ELA tests for their relevant grade level. This step required a fight with the federal department of education, which wanted California like other states to continue with the old tests for accountability purposes while the new tests were under development. But California leaders realized that this action would send mixed signals and incentives to schools and would delay real implementation efforts. They also believed an expanded field test would give teachers, students, and schools a relatively stress-free opportunity to experience the new test and to evaluate their technical capacity for full implementation the following year.

So they held firm, and the feds finally conceded.

Perhaps the stance of the governor and the state board of education was helped by an earlier action of the state legislature (2012) in which they explicitly moved away from simple test-based accountability by passing Senate Bill 1458. This amendment to the Public School Accountability Act of 1999 limits the weight allowed for test scores in the Academic Performance Index used for school accountability. This consistency across the legislative and executive branches has extended across multiple policy initiatives and reflects a growing sentiment for a new approach in the state.

As important as the policy steps the state *has* put in place are the steps it has chosen *not* to take. Most notable among these has been refusal to revise state teacher evaluation policies to incorporate teacher ratings based on student test scores. Citing state law that prohibits linking student outcome data to individual teachers, California resisted federal pressure and incentives to institute value-added educator evaluation processes. Even without this law, most stakeholders believe that such efforts would be premature and ill-advised. While taking this stance meant that the state has received neither a Race to the Top grant nor a waiver from NCLB accountability provisions, this decision has made it easier to keep the coalition of support for the Common Core together—something that has become increasingly difficult in jurisdictions where test-based accountability and evaluation have been confounded with implementation of the new standards.

## Lessons from California's Case

Several lessons emerge from the story of California's story of policy turnaround that may have implications for districts and other states as they move forward in their implementation efforts.

### Leadership

A key lesson here is the critical importance of leadership in establishing a policy environment conducive to the CCSS implementation. Several characteristics of that leadership in California stand out. It has been planned and systemic. At the outset, state board of education president Kirst mapped out the state systems that would need redirection to support CCSS implementation, and each of those has been and is being addressed. Additionally, while Kirst and the governor's office have played the central roles, the unity of purpose across the governor's office, legislature, and superintendent of public instruction has been unprecedented in recent state history and has enabled the work on all fronts to move forward. Equally important, state leaders have taken the long view on implementation, removing barriers, focusing on building system capacity, and extending the time to do so before instituting accountability measures. On this last note, they have also been courageous. They have eschewed both pressure and incentives to fall in line with a federal direction on student testing and teacher evaluation that they believed was not in the best interest of California's long-term goals.

## Constituency and Stakeholder Engagement

The depth of the shift embodied in the CCSS and the need for sustained implementation over time underscore the importance of a strong and engaged constituency and coordinated efforts among stakeholder groups. Mobilization of stakeholder groups in support of finance reforms built a basic foundation of trust and shared interest that has transferred in many cases to continued activity in support of Common Core. Indeed, many of the key activists for the Local Control Funding Formula are part of a growing consortium of stakeholders that have been working to expand and coordinate support for the Common Core. In addition, ongoing networking across local systems and between researchers, practitioners, and policymakers over the past ten years has also added to the social capital needed for systemic learning and improvement. In some cases this networking has led to formal partnerships like that of the ten CORE districts,[3] which have informed implementation efforts in other jurisdictions in the state. Finally, disentangling the CCSS in early stages of implementation from test-based accountability and teacher evaluation has allowed California to sustain support among stakeholders, particularly the teachers unions, when other jurisdictions are seeing such support diminish and in some cases disappear altogether.

## Adequacy and Equity of Resources

Without adequate and equitable resources, full implementation of CCSS would simply not occur. The needed steps toward this goal will obviously differ across states and even across districts within states. And California still has a long way to go to reach full adequacy. But the steps forward are promising and have sent a message of support and determination to local educators and other stakeholders alike.

*Flexibility and Coherence*

California's story is in many ways one of rebalancing the tension between policy coherence and local flexibility. Early versions of standards-based systemic reform argued for an approach to educational improvement that integrated top-down direction and support with bottom-up innovation and responsiveness to local conditions (Smith & O'Day, 1990). But subsequent reform efforts in California and across the nation moved increasingly in the direction of prescriptive mandates and heavy-handed accountability. We now have the opportunity to rebalance the scales, and California (among other states) has embarked on a journey to do just that.

## GOING THROUGH THE WINDOW

Creating a window of opportunity does not guarantee that California will take full advantage of that window to exit the traps of the past and transition smoothly to full CCSS implementation. Indeed, California faces several challenges moving forward, many of which have also emerged in other state and local systems.

First, while organized stakeholder groups are strongly on board, the broad public in California still knows little about the standards and is subject to negative narratives on the national scene. To date, there has been too little communication beyond organized groups about why the CCSS is needed in California, how it will impact students and their parents, and what is needed for implementation over the long haul.

Second, it is not clear that the local planning processes put in place for the Local Control Funding Formula will generate the kinds of strategic coherence and consistency needed to ensure deep implementation of instructional shifts called for by the standards. Indeed, CCSS is only one of eight state priorities that districts must address, and many districts lack the capacity to make necessary connections among those priorities or between them and their resource allocation decisions. In addition, the level of trust between equity advocates and local educators is still inchoate, and the funding formula remains an experiment in the eyes of many. The pullback to categorical streams and requirements will be strong, particularly if results for traditionally underserved students are insufficiently transparent or compelling.

Third, the accountability structures for both the Local Control Funding Formula and the Academic Performance Index are still being worked out. Many questions remain. How will the district-level criteria and rubrics align with measures put in place for schools? Who will set the targets and how will they balance support for improvement with intervention in case of failure?

And this brings us to the fourth and greatest challenge of all: How do we build both the individual and organizational capacity at the local level to enable the instructional shifts in classrooms across the state? Part of this challenge is resources and the still-inadequate funding for education in the state. Some of it is curricular and instructional materials. But the bulk of it is figuring out how to develop the deep levels of content knowledge and pedagogical skills needed for teachers to meet the instructional expectations of the Common Core. As one of the most successful local superintendents in the state has observed, "You'll never be better than your teachers." Yet California has almost three hundred thousand teachers, and they carry the burden for the success of the CCSS. Establishing the infrastructure to support them in this transition to the Common Core is an unprecedented challenge in the state and one that has yet to be fully addressed.

Implementing the Common Core is a long-term endeavor. At the moment there is political support in California and a generally conducive policy environment. But the state is still only at the beginning of the journey, and the policy window is fragile. The next few years will require vigilance—and restraint—at the state level to provide local educators with the space, resources, and help they need to climb through the window to enter an education future focused on improvement, learning, and student success.

## NOTES

1. These figures use eligibility for free and reduced-price lunches as a proxy for low income. Data for California come from the California Department of Education Data Quest figures for 2013/2014. The national figure is taken from the Southern Education Foundation (2013) and pertains to 2011 enrollment.

2. The Urban Education Dialogue, formed in 2000, is a learning community of superintendents from medium- to large-sized districts in California who meet three times annually to share strategies for educational improvement and equity. The California Collaborative on District Reform, formed in 2006, joins district leaders, researchers, state policymakers, funders, and other stakeholders in ongoing problem solving and collective action to improve instruction and outcomes for all students through systemic reform at the district level.

3. The California Office to Reform Education—or CORE, as most people refer to it—is a partnership of ten (mostly large urban) districts in the state that collectively serve over one million students. A cornerstone of CORE's work has been cross-district collaboration to support CCSS implementation in the member districts.

# References

Achieve, Inc. (2011). *Strong support, low awareness: Public perception of the Common Core State Standards.* Washington, DC: Author. Retrieved October 21, 2014, from www.achieve.org/PublicPerceptionCCSS.

Achieve, Inc. (2012). *Growing awareness, growing support: Teacher and voter understanding of the Common Core State Standards and Assessments.* Washington, DC: Author. Retrieved October 21, 2014, from www.achieve.org/growingawarenessCCSS.

Achieve, Inc. (2014). *Voter perceptions: Common Core State Standards and Tests.* Washington, DC: Author. Retrieved October 21, 2014, from www.achieve.org/publications/voter-perceptions-common-core-state-standards-tests.

Adamson, F., & Darling-Hammond, L. (2012). Funding disparities and the inequitable distribution of teachers: Evaluating sources and solutions. *Education Policy Analysis Archives, 20,* 37.

American Radio Works. (2014). *Greater expectations: The challenge of the Common Core.* Retrieved October 25, 2014, from www.americanradioworks.org/documentaries/greater-expectations/.

Anderson, J. (1988). *The education of blacks in the south, 1860–1935.* Chapel Hill: University of North Carolina Press.

Applebee, A. N. (1993). *Literature in the secondary school: Studies of curriculum and instruction in the United States.* Urbana, IL: National Council of Teachers of English.

Applebee, A. N., Burroughs, R., & Stevens, A. S. (1994). *Shaping conversations: A study of continuity and coherence in high school literature curricula* (Report Series 1.11). Albany, NY: National Research Center on Literature Teaching and Learning.

Applebee, A. N., & Langer, J. A. (2013). *Writing instruction that works.* New York: Teachers College Press.

Applebee, A. N., Langer, J. A., Nystrand, M., & Gamoran, A. (2003). Discussion-based approaches to developing understanding: Classroom instruction and student performance in middle and high school English. *American Educational Research Journal 40* (3), 685–730.

Ayres, L. P. (1909). *Laggards in our schools: A study of retardation and elimination in city school systems.* New York: Survey Associates & Russell Sage Foundation.

Bahr, D. L., & de Garcia, L. A. (2010). *Elementary mathematics is anything but elementary.* Independence, KY: Cengage Learning.

Ball, A. (2002). Three decades of research on classroom life: Illuminating the classroom communicative lives of America's at-risk students. In W. G. Secada (ed.), *Review of Reseach in Education 26* (pp. 71–112). Washington, DC: American Educational Research Association.

Ball, D. L., & Feiman-Nemser, S. (1988). Using textbooks and teachers' guides: A dilemma for beginning teachers and teacher educators. *Curriculum Inquiry 18* (4), 401–423.

180                                      *References*

Barnard, H. (1846). *Report on the condition and improvement of the public schools of Rhode Island, 1845.* Providence, RI: B. Cranston.

Berman, P., & McLaughlin, M. W. (1978). *Federal programs supporting educational change.* Vol. 8, *Implementing and sustaining innovations* (No. R-1589/8-HEW). Santa Monica, CA: RAND.

Bestor, A. E. (1953). *Educational wastelands: The retreat from learning in our public schools.* Urbana, IL: University of Illinois.

Bidwell, C. E. (2001). Analyzing schools as organizations: Long-term permanence and short-term change. *Sociology of Education, Extra Issue 2001*, 100–114.

Bryk, A., Sebring, P., Allensworth, E., Luppescu, S., & Easton, J. Q. (2010). *Organizing schools for improvement: Lessons from Chicago.* Chicago: University of Chicago Press.

Bunch, G. C., Kibler, A. K., & Pimentel, S. (2012). *Realizing opportunities for English learners in the Common Core English language arts and disciplinary literacy standards.* Stanford, CA: Understanding Language.

Calderon, M., Slavin, R., & Sanchez, M. (2011). Effective instruction for English learners. *Immigrant Children 21* (1), 103–128.

Camera, L. (2014). Oklahoma, Louisiana center stage in Common-Core fight. *Education Week 21* (September 10).

Christoph, J. N., & Nystrand, M. (2001). Taking risks, negotiating relationships: One teacher's transition toward a dialogic classroom. *Research in the Teaching of English 36*, 249–286.

City School Systems. (1890). *Journal of Proceedings and Addresses of the National Education Association*, 447–468.

Coburn, C. E. (2004). Beyond decoupling: Rethinking the relationship between the institutional environment and the classroom. *Sociology of Education*, 77(3), 211–244.

Cohen, D. K., Peurach, D. J., Glazer, J. L., Gates, K., & Goldin, S. (2014). *Improvement by design: The promise of better schools.* Chicago: University of Chicago Press.

Coleman, D., & Pimentel, S. (2012). Revised publishers' criteria for the Common Core State Standards in English language arts and literacy, grades 3–12. Common Core State Standards Initiative. Retrieved from http://www.corestandards.org/assets/Publishers_Criteria_for_3-12.pdf.

Committee of Ten. (1893). *Report of the Committee on Secondary School Studies appointed at the meeting of the National Education Association, 1892.* Washington, DC: Government Printing Office.

Conley, D. T. (2007). *Toward a more comprehensive conception of college readiness.* Eugene, OR: Educational Policy Improvement Center.

Council of Chief State School Officers. (2000). *Key state education policies on K–12 education: 2000.* Washington, DC: Author.

*Course of study for the common schools of Kansas.* (1907). Topeka, KS: Crane.

Crisis in education. (1958). *Life 44* (12) (March 24), 25–37.

Cuban, L. (2013). *Inside the black box of classroom practice: Change without reform in American education.* Cambridge, MA: Harvard Education Press.

Darling-Hammond, L. (2010). *The flat world and education: How America's commitment to equity will determine our future.* New York: Teachers College Press.

Darling-Hammond, L. (2014). Beyond the bubble test: Why we need performance assessments. *Education Week* (July 9). Retrieved from http://blogs.edweek.org/edweek/education_futures/2014/07/beyond_the_bubble_test_why_we_need_performance_assessments.html.

Darling-Hammond, L., Chung, R., & Frelow, F. (2002). Variation in teacher preparation: How well do different pathways prepare teachers to teach? *Journal of Teacher Education 53* (4), 286–302.

Darling-Hammond, L., & Post, L. (2000). Inequality in teaching and schooling: Supporting high-quality teaching and leadership in low-income schools. In Richard D. Kahlenberg (Ed.), *A notion at risk: Preserving public education as an engine for social mobility* (127–167). Washington, D.C.: Century Foundation Press.

Delpit, L. (1995). *Other people's children: Cultural conflict in the classroom.* New York: New Press.

Diamond, J. B. (2007). Where the rubber meets the road: Rethinking the connection between high stakes accountability policy and classroom instruction. *Sociology of Education 80* (4), 285–313.

Diamond, J. B. (2013). The resource and opportunity gap: The continued significance of race for African American student outcomes. In D. J. C. Andrews and F. Tuitt (eds.), *Contesting the Myth of a Post-Racial Era: The Continued Significance of Race in Education.* New York: Peter Lang.

Duncombe, W., & Yinger, J. (2007). *Understanding the incentives in California's education finance system. Getting Down to Facts.* Stanford, CA: Institute for Research on Education Policy and Practice.

Editorial Projects in Education Research Center. (2006). *Quality counts at 10: A decade of standards-based education.* Bethesda, MD: Author.

Elmore, R. F. (1996). Getting to scale with good educational practice. *Harvard Educational Review 66* (1), 1–27.

Evans, R. (1996). *The human side of school change: Reform, resistance, and the real-life problems of innovation.* Jossey-Bass Education Series. San Francisco: Jossey-Bass.

Fensterwald, J. (2014). Latest—but outdated—*Ed Week* survey ranks California 50th in per pupil spending. *EdSource Today* (January 14).

Finley, M. K. (1984). Teachers and tracking in a comprehensive high school. *Sociology of Education 57,* 233–243.

Fuller, B. (ed.). (2000). *Inside charter schools: The paradox of radical decentralization.* Cambridge, MA: Harvard University Press.

Fuller, B. (2010). Palace revolt in Los Angeles: Charter school and Latino leaders push unions to innovate. *Education Next 10.* Retrieved from http://educationnext.org/palace-revolt-in-los-angeles/.

Fuller, B. (in press). *Organizing locally: How the new decentralists improve education, health care, and trade.* Chicago: University of Chicago Press.

Fuller, B., Dauter, L., & Waite, A. (in press). New roles for teachers in diverse schools. In C. Bell & D. Gitomer (eds.), *Handbook of Research on Teaching.* New York: Routledge and American Education Research Association.

Fuller, B., & Parker, L. (in press). The four Rs: A charter school where relationships come first. In B. Fuller (ed.), *Organizing Locally: How the New Decentralists Improve Education, Health Care, and Trade.* Chicago: University of Chicago Press.

Fuller, B., Waite, A., Chao, C., & Benedicto, I. (2014). *Rich communities in small high schools? Teacher collaboration and cohesion in 25 Los Angeles campuses.* Berkeley: University of California, Graduate School of Education.

Gamoran, A., Secada, W. G., & Marrett, C. B. (2000). The organizational context of teaching and learning: Changing theoretical perspectives. In M. T. Hallinan (ed.), *Handbook of Research in the Sociology of Education* (pp. 37–63). New York: Kluwer Academic/Plenum.

Gándara, P., Maxwell-Jolly, J., & Driscoll, A. (2005). *Listening to teachers of English language learners: A survey of California teachers' challenges, experiences, and professional development needs.* Santa Cruz, CA: Center for the Future of Teaching and Learning.

Gewertz, C. (2014). Two districts, two approaches to Common-Core Curriculum. *Education Week 33* (29), 26–29. Retrieved on January 2, 2015, from www.edweek.org/ew/articles/2014/04/23/29cc-curriculum.h33.html?qs=two+districts+two+approaches.

Glazer, J. L., & Peurach, D. P. (2013). School improvement networks as a strategy for large-scale education reform: The role of environments. *Educational Policy 27* (4), 676–710.

Goldman, S. R., & Lee, C. (2014). Text complexity: State of the art and the conundrums it raises. *Elementary School Journal 115* (2).

Goldsworthy, H., Supovitz, J., & Riggan, M. (2013). *The lived experience of standards implementation in New York City schools, 2011.* Philadelphia, PA: Consortium for Policy Research in Education.

Goodlad, J. (2004). *A place called school: Twentieth anniversary edition.* New York: McGraw-Hill.

Gross, P., Buttrey, D., Goodenough, U., Koertge, N., Lerner, L. S., Schwartz, M., & Schwartz, R. (2013). *Final evaluation of the Next Generation Science Standards.* Washington, DC: Thomas B. Fordham Institute.

Guskey, T. R. (1986). Staff development and the process of teacher change. *Educational Researcher 15* (5), 5–12.

Guthrie, J. T., Schafer, W., Wang, Y. Y., & Afflerbach, P. (1995). Relationship of instruction to amount of reading: An exploration of social, cognitive, and instructional connections. *Reading Research Quarterly 30* (1), 8–25.

Gutiérrez, K. (2004). *Rethinking education policy for English learners.* Washington, DC: Aspen Institute.

Hatch, T. (2002). When improvement programs collide. *Phi Delta Kappan. 83* (8), 626–634.

Hatch, T. (2009). *Managing to change: How schools can survive (and sometimes thrive) in turbulent times.* New York: Teachers College Press.

Hatch, T. (2009). The outside-inside connection. *Educational Leadership, 67* (2), 16–21.

Hatch, T. (2013). Innovation at the core: What it really takes to improve classroom practice. *Phi Delta Kappan 95* (3), 34–38.

Hayton, P., & Spillane, J. P. (2008). Professional community or communities? School subject matter and elementary school teachers' work environments. In J. MacBeath and Y. C. Cheng (eds.), *Leadership for Learning: International Perspectives* (pp. 65–79). Rotterdam: Sense.

Heifetz, R. A., & Linsky, M. (2002). *Leadership on the line: Staying alive through the dangers of leading.* Vol. 465. Cambridge, MA: Harvard Business Press.

Heifetz, R. A., Linsky, M., & Grashow, A. (2009). *The practice of adaptive leadership: Tools and tactics for changing your organization and the world.* Cambridge, MA: Harvard Business Press.

Herold, B., & Molna, M. (2014). Research questions Common Core claims by publishers. *Education Week* (March 3). Retrieved from www.edweek.org/ew/articles/2014/03/05/23textbooks_ep.h33.html.

Hodge, E., & Benko, S. (2014). A common vision of instruction? An analysis of English/language arts professional development materials related to the Common Core State Standards. *English Teaching: Practice and Critique 13* (1), 169–196.

Honig, M., & Hatch, T. (2004). Crafting coherence: How schools strategically manage multiple, external demands. *Educational Researcher 33* (8), 16–30.

Hopkins, M., & Lowenhaupt, R. (2013). *Organizing language instruction in new immigrant destinations: Structural marginalization and integration.* Paper presented at the Segregation, Immigration, and Educational Inequality Conference, cosponsored by the Civil Rights Project, Ghent University, Université Libre de Bruxelles, and the UCLA Graduate School of Education and Information Studies, Ghent, Belgium.

Hopkins, M., Spillane, J. P., Jakopovic, P., & Heaton, R. (2013). Infrastructure redesign and instructional reform in mathematics: Formal structure and teacher leadership. *Elementary School Journal 114* (2).

Jackson, K. C., & Bruegmann, E. (2009). Teaching students and teaching each other: The importance of peer learning for teachers. *American Economic Journal: Applied Economics 1* (4), 85–108.

Kaestle, C. F. (1983). *Pillars of the republic: Common schools and American society, 1780-1860.* New York: Hill & Wang.

Kandel, W. A., & Parrado, E. A. (2006). Hispanic population growth and public school response in two new south destinations. In H. A. Smith and O.J. Furuseth (eds.), *Latinos in the New South: Transformations of Place* (pp. 111–134). Burlington, VT: Ashgate.

Kelly, S. (2004). Are teachers tracked? On what basis and with what consequences. *Social Psychology of Education 7*, 55–72.

Langer, J. A. (2001). Beating the odds: Teaching middle and high school students to read and write well. *American Educational Research Journal 38* (4), 837–880.

Layton, L. (2013,). Pearson pays $7.7 million in Common Core settlement. *Washington Post* (December 13). Retrieved November 26, 2014, from www.washingtonpost.com/local/

education/pearson-pays-77-million-in-common-core-settlement/2013/12/13/77515bba-6423-11e3-aa81-e1dab1360323_story.html.

Lee, C. D. (2007). *Culture, literacy and learning: Taking bloom in the midst of the whirlwind.* New York: Teachers College Press.

Lee, C. D., & Spratley, A. (2009). *Reading in the disciplines and the challenges of adolescent literacy.* New York: Carnegie Foundation of New York.

Lee, O., Quinn, H., & Valdes, G. (2013). Science and language for English language learners in relation to Next Generation Science Standards and with implications for Common Core State Standards for English language arts and mathematics. *Educational Researcher 42* (4), 223–233.

Levine, P., Lopez, M. H., & Marcelo, K. B. (2008). Getting narrower at the base: The American curriculum after *NCLB.* Medford, MA: Center for Information and Research on Civic Learning and Engagement.

Lloyd, G. M. (1999). Two teachers' conceptions of a reform-oriented curriculum: Implications for mathematics teacher development. *Journal of Mathematics Teacher Education 2* (3), 227–252.

Loeb, S., Bryk, A., & Hanushek, E. (2008). Getting down to facts: School finance and governance in California. *Education Finance & Policy 3* (1), 1–19.

Lowenhaupt, R. (in press). State policy and school capacity in Wisconsin's new Latino diaspora. In E. Hamann, E. Murillo, and S. Wortham (eds.*), Revisiting Education in the New Latino Diaspora.* Westport, CT: Ablex.

Lynch, J. J., & Evans, B. (1963). *High school English textbooks: A critical examination.* Boston: Little, Brown.

Massachusetts. *Annual report of the secretary of the board of education.* (1838, 1841). Boston: Dutton & Wentworth.

Matsumura, L. C. (2005). *Creating high-quality classroom assignments.* Lanham, MD: Scarecrow Education.

McDermott, K. A. (2013). Interstate governance of standards and testing. In P. Manna and P. McGuinn (eds.), *Rethinking Education Governance for the Twenty-First Century: Overcoming the Structural Barriers to School Reform* (pp. 130–155)*.* Washington, DC: Brookings Institution Press.

McDonnell, L. M., & Weatherford, M. S. (2013). Organized interests and the Common Core. *Educational Researcher 42,* 488–497.

McLaughlin, M. W. (1987). Learning from experience: Lessons from policy implementation. *Educational Evaluation & Policy Analysis 9* (2), 171–178.

McMurrer, J. (2007). *NCLB year 5: Choices, changes, and challenges: Curriculum and instruction in the NCLB era.* Washington, DC: Center on Education Policy.

Meyer, P. (2014). The history of history standards. In F. M. Hess and M. Q. McShane (eds.), *Common Core Meets Education Reform: What It All Means for Politics, Policy, and the Future of Schooling* (pp. 118–139). New York: Teachers College Press.

Mihalakis, V. (2010). *An analysis of the conceptual coherence and opportunities for interpretation in tenth grade literature textbooks.* Unpublished doctoral dissertation, University of Pittsburgh.

Mill, J. S. (1861). *Considerations on representative government.* London: Parker, Son & Bourn.

Mills, S. C., & Ragan, T. J. (2000). A tool for analyzing implementation fidelity of an integrated learning system. *Educational Technology Research & Development 48* (4), 21–41.

Morton, B. A., & Dalton, B. (2007). *Changes in instructional hours in four subjects by public school teachers of grades 1 through 4.* Washington, DC: National Center for Education Statistics.

Moschkovich, J. N. (2012). *Mathematics, the Common Core, and language: Recommendations for mathematics instruction for ELs aligned with the Common Core.* Stanford, CA: Understanding Language.

Nash, G. B., Crabtree, C. A., & Dunn, R. E. (2000). *History on trial: Culture wars and the teaching of the past.* New York: Vintage Books.

National Center for Educational Statistics. (1999). *Schools and Staffing Survey (SASS) 1998–1999 Teacher Questionnaire.* Washington, DC: U.S. Department of Education.

National Center for Educational Statistics. (2000). *Schools and Staffing Survey (SASS) 1999–2000 Teacher Questionnaire.* Washington, DC: U.S. Department of Education.

National Center for Educational Statistics. (2004). *Schools and Staffing Survey (SASS) 2003–2004 Teacher Questionnaire.* Washington, DC: U.S. Department of Education.

National Council on Education Standards and Testing. (1992). *Raising standards for American education.* Washington, DC: Government Printing Office.

National Governors Association Center for Best Practices & Council of Chief State School Officers. (2010). *Common Core State Standards key shifts in English language arts.* Washington, DC: Authors.

NEA Research. (2013). *Rankings and estimates: Rankings of the states 2012 and estimates of school statistics 2013.* Washington, DC: National Education Association.

Newmann, F., King, M., & Youngs, P. (2000). Professional development that addresses school capacity: Lessons from urban elementary schools. *American Journal of Education 108* (4), 259–299.

Nystrand, M., & Gamoran, A. (1997). The big picture: The language of learning in dozens of English lessons. In M. Nystrand (ed.), *Opening dialogue: Understanding the dynamics of language and learning in the English classroom.* New York: Teachers College Press.

Pearson, P. D., & Hiebert, E. H. (2014). The state of the field: Qualitative analyses of text complexity. *Elementary School Journal 114* (4).

Peske, H. G., & Haycock, K. (2006). *Teaching inequality: How poor and minority students are shortchanged on teacher quality: A report and recommendations by the education trust.* The Education Trust.

Peurach, D. J. (2011). *Seeing complexity in public education: Problems, possibilities, and success for All.* New York: Oxford University Press.

Peurach, D. J., & Glazer, J. L. (2012). Reconsidering replication: New perspectives on large-scale school improvement. *Journal of Educational Change 13* (2), 155–190.

Peurach, D. J., Glazer, J. L., & Lenhoff, S. W. (2014). The developmental evaluation of school improvement networks. *Educational Policy* (November 20). DOI: 10.1177 / 0895904814557592.

Polikoff, M.S. (2014). *The alignment of textbooks to the Common Core.* Paper presented at the 2014 Annual Meeting of the American Educational Research Association, Philadelphia, Pennsylvania.

Polikoff, M. S., Zhou, N., & Campbell, S. E. (in press). Methodological choices in the content analysis of textbooks for measuring alignment with standards. *Educational Measurement: Issues and Practice.*

Porter, A. C., Polikoff, M. S., Zeidner, T., & Smithson, J. (2008). The quality of content analyses of state student achievement tests and state content standards. *Educational Measurement: Issues and Practice 27* (4), 2–14.

Pound, F. A. (1897). State control and state uniformity of text-books. *Report of the State School Commissioner of Georgia to the General Assembly for 1896*, 112–126.

Price, J., & Ball, D. L. (1997). There's always another agenda: Marshalling resources for mathematics reform. *Journal of Curriculum Studies 29*, 637–666.

Reckhow, S., & Snyder, J. D. (2014). The expanding role of philanthropy in education politics. *Educational Researcher 43* (4), 186–195.

Reed, D. S. (2009). Is there an expectations gap? Educational federalism and the demographic distribution of proficiency cut scores. *American Educational Research Journal 46*, 718–742.

Remillard, J. T. (2005). Examining key concepts in research on teachers' use of mathematics curricula. *Review of Educational Research 75* (2), 211–246.

Remillard, J. T., & Bryans, M. B. (2004). Teachers' orientations toward mathematics curriculum materials: Implications for teacher learning. *Journal of Research in Mathematics Education 35* (5), 352–388.

Remillard, J. T. & Heck, D. (2014). Conceptualizing the curriculum enactment process in mathematics education. *ZDM: The International Journal on Mathematics Education 46* (5), 705–718.

Resnick, L. B., & Nelson-LeGall, S. (1997). Socializing intelligence. In L. Smith, J. Dockrell, and P. Tomlinson (eds.), *Piaget, Vygotsky and Beyond* (pp. 145-158). London: Routledge.

Rice, J. M. (1893). *The public-school system of the United States.* New York: Century.

Rowan, B., Correnti, R. J., Miller, R. J., & Camburn, E. M. (2009). *School improvement by design: Lessons from a study of comprehensive school reform programs.* Philadelphia, PA: Consortium for Policy Research in Education.

Sahlberg, P. (2011). *Finnish lessons: What can the world learn from educational change in Finland?* New York: Teachers College Press.

Schattschneider, E. E. (1960). *The semi-sovereign people: A realist's view of democracy in America.* New York: Holt, Rinehart & Winston.

Schmidt, W., & Houang, R. (2012). Curricular coherence and the Common Core State Standards for mathematics. *Educational Researcher 41*, 294–308.

Smith, H. (1873). *The academy as an organic part of our system of public education.* Proceedings of the Annual Meeting of the New York State Teachers Association. Albany: University of the State of New York, 24–30.

Smith, M. S., & O'Day, J. (1990). Systemic school reform. Journal of Education Policy, 5(5), 233–267.

Snyder, T. D., & Dillow, S. A. (2013). *Digest of educational statistics, 2012.* NCES 2014–2015. Washington, DC: National Center for Educational Statistics.

Spillane, J. P. (2004). Towards a theory of leadership practice. *Journal of Curriculum Studies,* 36(1), 3-34.

Spillane, J. P. (2005). Primary school leadership practice: How the subject matters. *School Leadership & Management 25* (4), 383–397.

Spillane, J. P., & Burch, P. (2003). Elementary School Leadership Strategies and Subject Matter: Reforming Mathematics and Literacy Instruction. *Elementary School Journal,* 103(5): 519–536.

Spillane, J. P., & Burch, P. (2006). The institutional environment and instructional practice: Changing patterns of guidance and control in public education. In Heinz-Dieter Meyer & Brian Rowan (eds.), *The new institutionalism in education* (87–102). Albany, NY: SUNY Press.

Spillane, J. P., Diamond, J. B., Walker, L. J., Halverson, R., & Jita, L. (2001). Urban school leadership for elementary science instruction: Identifying and activating resources in an undervalued school subject. *Journal of Research in Science Teaching 38* (8), 918–940.

Spillane, J. P., & Hopkins, M. (2013). Organizing for instruction in education systems and organizations: How the school subject matters. *Journal of Curriculum Studies 45* (6), 721–747.

Spillane, J. P., Parise, L. M., & Sherer, J. Z. (2011). Organizational routines as coupling mechanisms: Policy, school administration, and the technical core. *American Educational Research Journal 48* (3), 586–620.

Stage, E. K., Asturias, H., Cheuk, T., Daro, P. A., & Hampton, S. B. (2013). Opportunities and challenges in Next Generation Standards. *Science 340* (6130), 276–277.

Stodolsky, S. (1988). *The subject matters: Classroom activity in mathematics and social studies.* Chicago: University of Chicago Press.

Stone, D. (2002). *Policy paradox: The art of political decision making.* Rev. ed. New York: W. W. Norton.

Supovitz, J. A. (2008). Implementation as iterative refraction. In J. A. Supovitz and E. H. Weinbaum (eds.), *The Implementation Gap: Understanding Reform in High Schools* (pp. 151–172). New York: Teachers College Press.

Supovitz, J. A., Fink, R., & Newman, B. (2014). From the inside in: An examination of Common Core knowledge and communication in schools. CPRE Working Paper. Philadelphia, PA: Consortium for Policy Research in Education.

Supovitz, J. A. & Spillane, J. P. (2015). *Challenging standards: Navigating conflict and building capacity in the era of the Common Core.* Lanham, MD: Rowman & Littlefield.

Tyack, D. (1974). *The one best system: A history of American urban education.* Cambridge, MA: Harvard University Press.

Valencia, S. W., Wixson, K., & Pearson, P. D. (2014). Putting text complexity in context: Refocusing on comprehension of complex text. *Elementary School Journal 115* (2), 270–289.

Weick, K. (1979). *The social psychology of organizing*. Reading, MA: Addison-Wesley.

Wilson, H. B. (1915). *The minimum essential in elementary school subjects*. Fourteenth yearbook of the National Society for the Study of Education, part I. Chicago: University of Chicago Press, 9–20.

Wu, H. (2011). Phoenix rising: Bringing the Common Core state mathematics standards to life. *American Educator* (Fall), 3–13.

Zehler, A. M., Adger, C., Coburn, C., Arteagoitia, I., Williams, K., & Jacobson, L. (2008). *Preparing to serve English language learner students: School districts with emerging English language learner communities* (REL 2008-No.049). Washington, DC: U.S. Department of Education, Institute of Education Sciences, National Center for Education Evaluation and Regional Assistance, Regional Educational Laboratory Appalachia.

# About the Authors

## EDITORS

**Jonathan A. Supovitz** is the co-director of the Consortium for Policy Research in Education (CPRE) and a professor at the University of Pennsylvania's Graduate School of Education. His research examines the policy and leadership influences on the design and implementation of school improvement efforts.

**James P. Spillane** is the Spencer T. and Ann W. Olin Professor in Learning and Organizational Change at the School of Education and Social Policy at Northwestern University. He is also professor of Human Development and Social Policy, professor of Learning Sciences, professor of Management and Organizations, and faculty associate at Northwestern's Institute for Policy Research. His work explores the policy implementation process at the state, district, school, and classroom levels, focusing on intergovernmental and policy-practice relations.

## CONTRIBUTING AUTHORS

**Patricia Burch** is an associate professor at the Rossier School of Education at the University of Southern California. Burch studies the patterns and drivers of school commercialism and the implications for the form and delivery of public education, with specific attention to equity and quality.

**John B. Diamond** is the Hoefs-Bascom Professor of Education at the University of Wisconsin–Madison. Diamond is a sociologist of education who focuses on how race, ethnicity, and social class intersect with school practices and policies to determine the educational opportunities and outcomes of children.

**Bruce Fuller** is a professor of education and public policy at the University of California–Berkeley. Fuller's current research delves into how young children are socialized in diverse Mexican-American homes, and what neighborhood organizations effectively advance their development.

**David A. Gamson** is an associate professor of education in the Department of Education Policy Studies at the Pennsylvania State University. Gamson's research focuses on educational policy and school reform, past and present. Recently, he examined the evolving roles and responsibilities of the school district since World War II.

**Annalee Good** is an associate researcher at the Wisconsin Center for Education Research. Good's current projects include studies of digital tools in K–12 supplemental education, academic tutoring partnerships, and the challenges of instruction and assessment for advanced learners.

**Thomas Hatch** is an associate professor of education at Teachers College, Columbia University, and co-director of the National Center for Restructuring Education, Schools, and Teaching (NCREST). Hatch's research focuses on creating methods and resources that support the examination of teaching at all levels and issues of large-scale school reform.

**Emily Hodge** is an assistant professor of educational leadership at Montclair State University. She received her PhD from the Educational Theory and Policy program at the Pennsylvania State University. Hodge's research explores how educational systems, schools, and teachers negotiate the tension between standardization and differentiation in the context of Common Core implementation.

**Megan Hopkins** is an assistant professor of education at the Penn State College of Education. Hopkins's research examines the relationships between educational policy, teacher education, and school and classroom practice in the context of policy and/or demographic change.

**Andrew L. LaFave** is a PhD student in K–12 urban education policy at the University of Southern California Rossier School of Education. His current research focuses on the schools as organizations and the power dynamics that exist between and among administrators, teachers, and students.

**Carol D. Lee** is the Edwina S. Tarry Professor of Education in the School of Education and Social Policy and in African American studies at Northwestern University. Lee's research addresses cultural supports for learning that include a broad ecological focus, with attention to language and literacy and African American youth.

**Kathryn A. McDermott** is associate professor of education and public policy and acting director of the Center for Public Policy and Administration for the 2013/2014 academic year. McDermott conducts research on the formation and implementation of state-level education policy and the effects of policy on educational equity.

**Patrick McGuinn** is associate professor of political science at Drew University. McGuinn's research interests are in national politics and institutions, education and social welfare policy, American political development, federalism, and the policymaking process.

**Vivian Mihalakis** is a senior fellow in English language arts/literacy at the Institute for Learning at the Learning Research and Development Center at the University of Pittsburgh. She also teaches at the University of Pittsburgh's Graduate School of Education. Her work includes designing educative ELA/literacy curriculum, performance assessments, and professional development.

**Jennifer A. O'Day** is an Institute Fellow at American Institutes for Research. O'Day has carried out research, advised national and state policymakers, and written extensively in the areas of systemic standards-based reform, educational equity, accountability, and capacity-building strategies. Her recent work focuses on strategies for intervening in low-performing, high-poverty schools identified under systems of state, local, and federal accountability.

**Anthony Petrosky** is the associate dean of the School of Education at the University of Pittsburgh, holds a joint appointment as a professor in the School of Education and the English department. Petrosky co-directs the English Language Arts Disciplinary Literacy Project in the Institute for Learning (IFL) at the Learning Research and Development Center. As a part of this institute project, he has worked with professional learning and curriculum development in English for school and district leaders in the public schools of Austin, Dallas, Denver, New York City, Fort Worth, Prince George's County, and Pittsburgh.

**Donald J. Peurach** is an assistant professor at the University of Michigan School of Education and teaches courses in educational administration and policy, and educational leadership and policy. Peurach's research sits at the intersection of educational organization, reform, and policy and is focused on devising methods of collaborating with network leaders to improve ways in which their enterprises function as learning systems that improve and adapt over time.

**Morgan S. Polikoff** is an assistant professor of education at the Rossier School of Education at the University of Southern California. Polikoff's areas of expertise include K–12 education policy; Common Core standards; assessment policy, alignment among instruction, standards, and assessments; and the measurement of classroom instruction.

**Janine Remillard** is one of the primary faculty in the Teacher Education Program and in the Teaching, Learning, and Leadership Division at the University of Pennsylvania Graduate School of Education. Remillard has directed a number of studies focusing on mathematics teaching and curriculum in the United States and regularly participates in cross-national exchanges on teaching and teacher education, most recently with educators from China and South Korea.

**Joshua Taton** is a doctoral candidate in teaching, learning, and curriculum at the University of Pennsylvania's Graduate School of Education. In addition to his work on the iCubit project, his research experiences have also involved teacher preparation in cross-cultural contexts, distributed leadership, professional learning communities, and educational technology.